Here I Am, Lord—
Send Someone Else

To order additional copies of
Here I Am, Lord—Send Someone Else,
by Curtis DeWitt, call **1-800-765-6955**.

Visit us at
www.reviewandherald.com
for information on other Review and Herald® products.

Here I Am, Lord—
Send
Someone Else

CURT DeWITT

REVIEW AND HERALD® PUBLISHING ASSOCIATION
Since 1861 | www.reviewandherald.com

Published by Review and Herald® Publishing Association, Hagerstown, MD 21741-1119

Review and Herald® titles may be purchased in bulk for educational, business, fund-rais-
ing, or sales promotional use. For information, please e-mail SpecialMarkets@reviewand-
herald.com.

The Review and Herald® Publishing Association publishes biblically based materials for
spiritual, physical, and mental growth and Christian discipleship.

The author assumes full responsibility for the accuracy of all facts and quotations as cited
in this book.

Unless otherwise noted, all Bible texts in this book are from the New King James
Version. Copyright © 1979, 1980, 1982 by Thomas Nelson, Inc. Used by permission.
All rights reserved.

Bible texts credited to RSV are from the Revised Standard Version of the Bible,
copyright © 1946, 1952, 1971, by the Division of Christian Education of the National
Council of the Churches of Christ in the U.S.A. Used by permission.
Scripture quotations marked NLT are taken from the *Holy Bible,* New Living
Translation, copyright © 1996. Used by permission of Tyndale House Publishers, Inc.,
Wheaton, Illinois 60189. All rights reserved.
Verses marked TLB are taken from *The Living Bible,* copyright © 1971 by Tyndale
House Publishers, Wheaton, Ill. Used by permission.

This book was
Edited by Penny Estes Wheeler
Cover designed by Trent Truman
Cover art by JupiterImages
Typeset: Bembo 12/14.5

PRINTED IN U.S.A.

11 10 09 08 07   5 4 3 2 1

Library of Congress Cataloging-in-Publication Data
DeWitt, Curtis, 1965-   .
  Here I Am, Lord—Send Someone Else / Curtis DeWitt.
    p. cm.
  ISBN 978-0-8280-1942-2
  1. DeWitt, Curtis, 1965-   .   2. Missionaries—Kenya—Biography.   3. Seventh-day
Adventists—Biography.   4. Adventists—Biography.   5. Sabbatarians—
Biography.   I. Title.
  BV3625.K42D49 2007
  266'.67092—dc22
  [B]
                                                        2007004910

In Memory

This book was written
in memory of my mother,
Betty Jean DeWitt,
who was killed in a car accident in 1993.
I have sorely missed her all these years,
but can't wait to share these stories with her
when, hopefully, we embrace once again in heaven.

Special Thanks

To my wife, Kim, who finally convinced me to go to Africa. I couldn't have made it without you. Now I truly understand why tears so often filled your beautiful eyes as you longed to go back home to Kenya.

To my children: Stephanie, Stephen, and Ashley. You made Africa extraspecial. You kept our home lively and energetic, and together we created wonderful memories that we will remember forever. I'm so proud of each of you!

To my dad, Harold DeWitt, for your constant love-filled prayers and listening ear over those six years. You will never know just how much your prayers and encouraging love gave me strength to keep moving forward.

To my siblings: Cindy Hall, Cathy DeWitt, and Craig DeWitt. It was difficult being away from you for so long, but knowing that one day I would return and we could be together again like the days of old kept my spirits up and running.

To my in-laws, Norman and Beverly Pottle, who gave us so much support. You understand a lot of our trials as long ago you were missionaries yourselves. Your consistent, encouraging e-mails were a bright light during our days.

To the Maxwell Adventist Academy staff and students. You were a huge part of my life during our time in Kenya. I will never, ever forget you and I hope we will meet again—if not on earth, then in that special place God has prepared for us.

To Jesus Christ, my personal Savior, to whom I owe everything. You carried me when I couldn't walk. You loved me unconditionally no matter my failures. Thank You for this time in my life. No sacrifice is too great for You!

Contents

Foreword

Walking to the administration building one morning, I noticed two students running around behind the church. I quickly saw that they were of the opposite sex, so I thought I had better go and check it out, because you never know what a young man and woman might be planning even if they're right next to the church.

As I rounded the side of the building I saw them near the side door. And no, they weren't kissing or even holding hands. In fact, I think they were completely oblivious to each other's presence. "Hey, guys," I said. "What's up?"

None too calmly Nick Delgado quickly retorted, "A snake! A snake, Pastor Curt! It just went under the door into the church."

"Could you tell what kind it was?" I asked. I felt a little excited myself. I'd wanted to see a snake in Africa ever since I was about 5 years old.

"I'm pretty sure it was a spitting cobra!"

★ ★ ★

Take note that at the beginning of each chapter is a key text.

This key text is a scripture that I have written in my own words and it applies to the particular situation you'll read about in that chapter. I've placed the initials PCRV after these texts. PCRV stands for *Pastor Curt's revamped version*.

Introduction

I once adamantly stated that I would *never* be a pastor and *definitely* not a missionary! On top of that, I was, to put it mildly, afraid of teenagers. But God had other plans, which all began with the tragic death of my mother. A few years later I found myself in Africa, a missionary pastor working with teenagers! What an experience it was, and I wouldn't trade it for the world today. In this book I share some of my life's experiences, most of which occurred during our missionary journey in Kenya. After reading this book, you will see how God led step by step all along my life's way, and how He helped me overcome my fears. My experiences taught me some valuable lessons and hopefully you too will grasp the spiritual lessons God taught me.

God works in so many marvelous and sometimes mysterious ways and when I look back on my life I just shake my head in amazement. Even when God allows tragedy in a person's life, He turns it into a blessing. One very important lesson I learned throughout our time in Kenya is that when you put your life into God's hands, you had better fasten your seat belt and hang on. You never know where God will take you and how you will ever make it to your destination. But in the end, if you trust your Father, He will carry you through it all.

Truly "anything that can happen will happen" in Kenya, as you will see after reading this book. Whether it deals with capturing a spitting cobra in church, people-eating lions, setting up circumstances to catch thieves, or spiritually wrestling with the powers of darkness for the life of a student, you will see how the amazing hand of God moved in my life and in the lives of others. Most important, I hope that you will understand how He is intimately involved in your own life. I hope and pray that God will guide your thoughts as you see how He led my life every step of the way.

Chapter 1

The Day I Tried to Kill Jesus

We know that everything works for our good when we love God, especially the tragic things that turn our world upside down. The day I lost my mother in a car accident God turned my life around so He and I could have a close relationship. Then came the time He called me to do something I would never have done had not my mother died sometime before (Romans 8:28, PCRV).

Michigan, 1993

I'll never forget that hot July day as long as I live. My wife and I were at her parents' home, relaxing out in the sun while our kids played in a kiddie pool. We were talking about our upcoming move to Coldwater, Michigan, where I'd accepted a job as head teacher for the elementary school. Life was good. The day was beautiful, and I was relaxed and happy about moving to the town where my parents lived.

As it neared suppertime my wife, Kim, decided that hot dogs sounded good, so she asked me if I'd go down the road to Apple Valley Market and pick up some buns. So I took off even happier because I love hot dogs and I lived to eat. I bought the buns and headed back home looking forward to a tasty meal. Carefree, I pulled into the driveway and stepped out of the car. Before I took even three steps I saw Kim running toward me, a terrible look on her face. I'd never seen such a look before, but I knew that it meant something bad.

"Something terrible has happened!" she gasped, her voice strained and broken.

Instantly my heart began to race as my mind leaped to the conclusion that something had happened to my dad. Dad had problems with his back, and had had a few surgeries on some ruptured disks, so I figured it must be him.

"What's wrong? What happened?"

Nothing could have prepared me for what came out of Kim's mouth next.

"Your mom's been killed in a terrible car accident," she said, tears streaming down her cheeks.

"What? That's impossible! No way!" My brain went into an immediate meltdown. "I'm going to call my dad!"

It was impossible to accept. It was ridiculous. Words didn't make it true. I'd call my dad, and he'd tell me my mom was OK.

Turning away from Kim, I marched into the house and bounded up the stairs. Along the way I noticed my mother-in-law sitting on the couch crying quietly, her head slightly down. In that moment I was seized by a blinding rage and a powerful desire to grab her and throw her through the window. My mother-in-law and I had a good relationship. There was no animosity between us at all. This weird impulse came from this ugly situation. At that moment I hated her—because she was alive while my mom was dead.

Only by the grace of God was I able to stifle my rage and keep on walking. At the same time, my mind rejected Kim's message, and I stomped up to the bedroom, where I could call my dad in private. I picked up the phone and punched the numbers. My heart raced and my breath came shallow even as I prayed and mentally tried to will the inevitable away. The phone rang twice. When I heard Dad's trembling hello, reality struck like a punch right in my stomach.

"Dad?" I said.

Tell me Kim is lying. Tell me it's not true.

"Dad?"

"Curt, oh, Curt! She's gone! Curt, Curt." My dad sobbed uncontrollably on the other end of the line as tears pressed their way into my eyes, and still I mentally refused to let it be true. I fought that sorrow as though my very life depended upon it. Quickly wiping away the tears, I told my dad that I'd be there as soon as I could. Then I went back downstairs and began packing my clothes. Kim implored me to let her go too, but I told her that I wanted to go alone. "Someone will need to watch the kids anyway," I asserted.

"Then ask Chris to go with you," she begged. Chris Davisson was a close friend of mine, but I didn't want him. I didn't want anyone. Finally Kim stopped pushing the matter, but driving alone after hearing devastating news of a death was a big mistake. Little did I realize the power of my emotions as they carried me along through this dark, endless tunnel of grief.

So I got in the car and began the hour-and-a-half trip to Coldwater. I started off OK, but about 15 miles down the road it suddenly felt like a huge bubble was rapidly expanding in my chest, until, at last, it reached the breaking point and a torrent of emotions exploded in a fit of anger and rage.

The scariest part of it was that for the first time in my life, I felt totally out of control. I pounded the steering wheel and screamed at the top of my lungs, *"Nnnnoooooooo!"* But again, my willpower was stronger than the emotions, and I was able to suppress those feelings. Pushing them as far back as I could, I quickly gained control and concentrated on driving. My glance darted around the car. I noticed the stereo and decided that I needed music, loud music, so that I couldn't hear myself think. Quickly I punched on a station of rock music and turned up the volume so loud that I literally couldn't hear my thoughts. I didn't normally listen to that kind of stuff, but at that point I didn't care about anything other than not accepting reality.

And so there I drove, the rock music screaming in my ears, drowning out any conscious thought. But again—about halfway to my parents' house—I suddenly felt the same bubble growing in my chest until it erupted in the same fashion. This time it was much harder to get it under control. After about a minute of raging and venting my frustration on the steering wheel, I fought to gain the upper hand. Somewhere, despite the raging music, I remember hearing a voice inside my mind imploring me to turn the radio off so God could help me.

But I didn't care about God at that point. I only wanted to escape my haunting thoughts.

On and on I drove, wishing I could go on forever so that I didn't have to drive up my parents' driveway and find Mom no longer there. The elementary school I'd planned to teach at was about two miles from my parents' house, and as I neared the school grounds I felt hatred for that school filling my heart. The emotion that poured forth this time was worse than the previous two times put together. As the school drew closer I started shouting at the top of my lungs. I even rolled down my window so the school could hear how much I hated it! I cursed that place with everything I had, using the worst possible four-letter words I could muster even as tears forced their way from my eyes and streamed down my cheeks. To this day, I am so thankful to God that nobody was at the school to hear my unchristian mouth during my terrible rage.

As I pulled up to my parents' home I saw other cars in the driveway. Talk about feeling numb and wishing I could be anywhere else in the world! As I walked up to the front porch the door suddenly opened and a couple of church members came out and hugged me. I know they were trying to show sympathy, but at that point, that was the last thing I needed. I needed to see my dad, and that was all. I walked into the house and went to my parents' bedroom, where I found Dad weeping uncontrollably as he looked at Mom's picture. We hugged, and I tried hard to be strong for him.

"Oh, Curt, she's gone! Curt, Curt . . ." Dad could hardly talk. I don't recall much else at that point, but somehow he calmed down enough to tell me what had happened. Mom had been driving her car from Battle Creek back toward home when she went through a stop sign. A woman coming from the other direction hit her broadside, right where Mom was sitting. She never had a chance, and most likely didn't even know what hit her. The accident report said that her neck was broken as well as bones inside her chest area. A blind boy, whom she took care of a couple days a week, was with her. He was mostly unhurt, and for that I was very grateful. The woman in the car that hit her had some damage to her leg. Again, I felt so thankful that God spared her life, too. An officer had stopped at the house to tell my dad the terrible news. Dad said that when the policeman said his piece he wanted to hit him. He, too, refused to believe the truth about his dearly loved wife.

Over the next 24 hours my siblings came to the house at different times, each struggling mightily to accept and adjust to their loss. When Cathy, the second-oldest, came in, she went throughout the house loudly calling for Mom, hoping that Mom would pop out of a back bedroom with welcoming arms. It tore my heart out to hear her. And so as she came hysterically down the hall still yelling for her mother, I grabbed her and held her close, even though she tried to break away. We wept together as I cried, "She's gone, Cath; she's gone."

Later that day we drove to a nearby service station where the wrecked vehicle had been towed. All of us were still desperately struggling with the reality of the situation and needed to see the car. Reaching the place, we had a difficult time getting in. The man in charge had been strictly told that nobody was to touch the car nor go anywhere near it, so he couldn't let us in. After we talked to him for 20 minutes, his heart was won over. We walked solemnly toward the car. There was no question that it had been in a terrible wreck. The driver's door was smashed in and the seat turned sideways. Even though Mom had been wearing her seat belt, it didn't help much. There was a lot of dried blood on the floor under the seat. We cried some more and had a hard time not imaging the impact of the crash as it crushed the life out of our loved one.

That Friday evening it was very difficult to go into the funeral home for the first time. I slowly walked into the carefully lit viewing room, hoping against hope that the body in the casket was not my mom's—that there had been some mistake. I stared into that small space looking at the distorted form of my dear mother. How could this be happening to me? to us? Where was God? How could I see His love through something so horrible as the death of my mom? She and I were so close. I cried and hugged her body, wishing with all my heart that she would hug me back, but of course it was to no avail. She was gone.

That Sabbath, the only day of visitation, was one of numb disbelief. All afternoon people came in and out of that funeral home offering their condolences, hugs, and tears. That day was the longest day
of my life, yet I never wanted it to end. Our relatives will never know
just how much it meant to me and my family that they were there for
us to lean upon. To have one of my aunts come over to me and encourage me to get something to eat, or have an uncle place his arm
around my shoulders and ask if I was OK, helped me feel so loved in
my deepest time of sorrow. I don't think I would have survived without them. I will never forget one gentleman, Clendon Hamilton, who
came at the earliest time possible and sat on a couch until closing. He
did nothing. He said not a word. He just sat sorrowfully, giving me
more support than nearly everybody else combined.

The funeral took place the next day, Sunday. Monday we drove
to Holly, Michigan, to bury her near some of our relatives. My dad,
my sisters and brothers, and I all took turns covering Mom's casket.
We wouldn't have had it any other way. No common worker was
going to throw dirt on our mother's face, so to speak. Oh, such
painful proceedings—where was God when I was suffering so
much? I couldn't feel Him with me. Where was He when the going
got tough? I was sure that He had gotten up and left me.

From that point on I began to fight a battle more terrible than the
initial shock of Mom's death. I battled anger continually. At times I
was so mad that I felt I could spit fire! I blamed Satan for my pain and
anguish and longed to go a couple of rounds with him. My anger
quickly turned into a hatred from which I felt there was no escape.

I wasn't used to not controlling my emotions. I'd be sitting
watching TV and suddenly something would remind me of my
mother and I'd get up and go into the bathroom to spill some tears.
As one can imagine, when special days came around—such as
Mom's birthday or Thanksgiving—about a week ahead of the actual
date I'd start feeling more and more irritable. When the actual day
arrived, all the inner turmoil of emotions that had been building up
would explode. I felt terrible for my wife and two kids. I knew I was
causing them pain, but I couldn't help myself.

The more time that passed, the angrier I became. I often thought of Satan and how I hated him. At night I'd dream that he stood in my doorway looking like my mom. In my dreams I always knew it was him, and I would start bashing him and throwing stuff at him until he was beaten into a small pancake. In my dream I would then go around gloating about how I had beaten the tar out of Satan. Sometimes those dreams repeated in a never-ending loop until they became nightmares, with Satan getting the upper hand. Many nights I lay awake, fearing that my mom would appear beside my bed. Night after night I feared to go to sleep, and because my hold on God was broken I felt that He couldn't help me. Yet I tried to pray. At night I read my Bible, looking for something to help me overcome my hatred and fear, but it did no good. My focal point was me, myself, and I, and that was it. I became so self-absorbed that it was simply impossible for me to get a grip on life.

I don't know how in the world I survived that school year, but I know again that God sent friends to help me survive. Bob and Darlene Huckabay looked for out both my dad and me. Darlene was my fellow teacher at the elementary school—a constant blessing, and so sensitive to our needs. Bob and Darlene were so kind. Their simply being my friends made all the difference and gave me courage to keep on going.

My wife, bless her heart, gave so much to me. I know it had to be difficult to give when I was not giving back to her in any way. Knowing how I struggled, she tried to be so patient and loving with me. I will never forget her love and her caring ways.

By day I threw myself into my teaching and did a pretty good job staying busy. But at night the devil haunted my dreams, and memories often swallowed me up. Whenever I talked to anyone about my struggles, I'd always say that Satan had caused this pain and that one day he would pay for it. I knew all the right answers from the Bible and felt sure that I was directing my anger toward Satan, where it belonged.

One of the more memorable things I decided to do was to build a chapel in back of the school, just inside the wooded area. It was a beautiful, peaceful setting. The students and I did some cleaning up, digging, and moving stumps until it was finished. We had a few rows of rough-hewn pews, and even a stump for a pulpit. To top it all off, we placed a rugged cross behind the pulpit. I remember a number of Saturday night vespers we held in that chapel in the woods. We even put up a sign in memory of my mom. It read *Betty Jean Chapel.* The whole area was quite special to me, and some days after school would find me just sitting there on one of the wooden pews, thinking.

But night after night my struggles continued, as I wrestled with my feelings. I was able to suppress them in the daylight hours, but fought an endless battle after dark. I knew that I couldn't go on like this much longer. Something had to give, or I would soon welcome death as my savior. My relationship with God was nonexistent, and it felt that Satan had his way with me whenever he felt like it. I knew that sooner or later God would have to step in and do something or his counterpart would destroy my life.

One day near the end of that first school year I had a particularly rough time teaching. At last school let out. The kids had gone home, and Darlene was away as well so I thought it was a good time to go sit in our little chapel in the woods. Sitting down on the front pew, I started thinking about the past school year. Suddenly I began to feel very strange inside my stomach—as if something were physically happening there. I had no idea what it was. To this day I remember that I experienced no conscious thought or previous plan for what happened next.

It was as if all the rage, anger, and frustration I'd forced down inside for the past year burst out in a ferocious storm. I jumped to my feet. Quickly looking around, I picked up a large rock—maybe 25 inches in circumference—turned to face the cross, then drew back my arm with all my strength. Then with an angry guttural yell I let that rock fly! It struck the cross with a resounding crack, right where the head of Jesus would have been.

Tears burst from my eyes as I realized what I'd just done. I had tried to kill Jesus, my Savior, the one who died on that lonely cross for me! I had sided with Satan in nailing Him there with hatred in my heart. I fell flat on the ground, scared to death that I was going to be struck down by lightning. I knew my life was over. I had committed the unpardonable sin in trying to crush the head of Jesus. Surely God could never forgive me—could He?

"God, forgive me!" I cried from the depths of my heart, fully expecting a flash of light that would end my life. "Please forgive me! Let me live! I'm sorry, I'm sorry!" I waited in terror, but it never came. *It never came.* After a few minutes, when I realized that I was still alive, I sat up and looked around. As I was staring at the cross, a thought hit me like a ton of bricks. All this time I had been angry at God, not Satan. It was God who could have stopped my mom from being killed. I knew that Satan was that kind of tyrant, one who was always out to hurt, maim, and kill people. I expected nothing less out of him, but God, *my loving God,* could have stepped in and prevented that car from snuffing out my mother's life. I had tried so hard to push my anger onto Satan's back, but it was God, not Satan, whom I felt had betrayed me.

"Why, God? Why did *You* let this happen?" I cried as I sat on the ground wiping my eyes. At last I pushed myself to my feet. I was emotionally drained. It was with more than a little thankfulness in my heart at still being alive that I went back to my car and headed home.

I found out more about God that day than I ever knew before. I realized that He is not the kind of God that waits around to catch people making mistakes and then zaps them with a thunderbolt. He is a God who loves at all costs, whether I return that love or not. Truly His love covers a multitude of sins (1 Peter 4:8), even the worst kind of sins. God knew that I needed to see the truth before He could mend my heart. Once I realized the truth about my feelings, then I was able to begin healing.

You know what the most amazing part of this whole incident is? Through those long terrible months after Mom died, God knew my hatred was really directed at Him, yet He never left me. He saw me throw that rock at that cross, yet He stayed by my side. You see, God is big enough to take rocks being thrown at Him. Yes, I hurt Jesus' feelings. I nailed Him once again to that same cross He suffered on so long ago, but He still loved me and was willing to wait until He could lead me out of my tunnel of darkness into His marvelous arms of love. Jesus has an abundance of mercy and long-suffering in His blood. He will wait patiently for us to come to our senses. Sometimes it's hard not being able to see through His eyes. We see so little that when extreme situations come our way, such as the death of a dear mother, all looks hopeless. If we could just get one glimpse through His eyes, we would quickly see that He's got everything under control and that He knows exactly what He is doing. He does care when good people die (see Psalm 116:15).

It took awhile for me to get an answer to my *why* questions, but now I understand why God allowed this great sadness to come into my life. I believe that one of the biggest reasons God allowed my mom to die was simply to turn my own spiritual life upside down! Up to that point, as I previously wrote, I didn't have a serious relationship with Him. I was doing my own thing, living for pleasure instead of living for Jesus Christ, my Savior. My mom died so that Jesus could save me, my brother, my two sisters, and my dad. I know that there were others as well who gave their lives to Jesus because of Mom's death. You see, God is in the saving business. To put it frankly, He will do anything it takes to save you and me—even allowing our loved ones to die, for He knows that we'll soon have all eternity to spend together.

How many times have others asked me such questions as Why does God allow this or that to happen to *me?* Why are babies born with AIDS? Why are little children sexually molested or beaten? Why are helpless women raped? Why do mothers die, leaving kids alone? Why do people suffer with cancer? Why? Why? Why?

God knows that if we taste of Satan's kingdom we will pull away from this world, because God's love is a whole lot better than Satan's wickedness, which does nothing but break our hearts. God also allows good people to die to spare them from crises down the road in their lives. Maybe my mom would have faced something that would have been too much for her to handle and she would have eternally fallen by the wayside.

Today, as I look back at my life, I humbly bow to my Father's wisdom and foreknowledge. Now I see what I deem the greatest reason God let my mother die. It was so my family and I could break away from all that was familiar and travel to the country of Kenya. God had a mission for me and my wife, but before He could accomplish His purposes He had to sever my relationship from someone near and dear to my heart. God knew that with my mother around, my ties with her were too strong for me to follow Him wherever He needed me to go. Without a doubt, if my mother had not died, I would never have become a pastor and definitely not a missionary, nor would I have worked with academy-age youth. I would have stayed in Coldwater, Michigan, content for a long time. It was only after Mom and I were forced to part on this earth that my life focus changed. After that accident I realized that there was only one thing that mattered, and that was drawing near to God and developing a saving relationship with Him. Only then could I willingly sacrifice my life for Him and go to Africa to point young people to Calvary.

What kind of God is the one we call Father? Exactly two years from the day that we buried my mom, our daughter Ashley was born—in spite of my having had a vasectomy. God lovingly placed His huge arms around me and said, "I love you, son! I'll give you someone else to love, someone who will help fill that large empty void until you meet your mother again when Jesus comes to take you home."

What kind of God is He? He's a God who loves me with all His heart, and you know what? He loves you in just the same way—as if there were no one else on the face of this planet! No matter what happens in your life, you can trust Him. "For I am persuaded that neither death nor life, nor angels nor principalities nor powers, nor things present nor things to come, nor height nor depth, nor any other created thing, shall be able to separate us from the love of God which is in Christ Jesus our Lord" (Romans 8:38, 39).

If you have lost a loved one and are having a hard time trusting God with it, let me remind you of some life-saving facts:

1. Your much-loved mother cannot be tempted by Satan any

longer. This is all I need to remember to bring a smile to my face when I'm missing my mom.

2. Your own dad is sleeping peacefully, and it will seem but a moment until he sees Jesus coming to take him home.

3. Your close brother's eternal destiny is forever fixed and held in God's hands.

4. Maybe God allowed your wife's death to save her from being eternally lost. You wouldn't have it any other way, would you? Reflect on the words found in Isaiah 57:1, 2: "The righteous perishes, and no man takes it to heart; merciful men are taken away, while no one considers *that the righteous is taken away from evil.* He shall enter into peace; they shall rest in their beds, each one walking in his uprightness."

5. God most likely turned others' lives around because of the death of your priceless child. You will see him or her in the kingdom, because your child died to save others.

6. When your sister died, it was Satan that caused your pain. Already God has lovingly planned a special reunion for you—as soon as you see Jesus' beautiful face coming in the clouds (see 1 Thessalonians 4:16, 17).

7. Maybe your husband died so that *you* would be saved. He wouldn't have had it any other way, would he?

Chapter 2

I Can't Believe I'm in Africa!

Trust God with everything, especially when you have to make a life-changing decision! Don't have any confidence in yourself or your own way of thinking. Keep God first in your life and let Him lead. Then watch Him tear down those walls that stand in your way (Proverbs 3:5, 6, PCRV).

I t seemed like only yesterday that we had decided to become missionaries to Kenya. I couldn't believe that we were on the huge 747 and only an hour away from touching down at the Kenyatta Airport in Nairobi. Thoughts raced through my head as I contemplated my life before we made the decision to leave everything that was familiar to go serve in a foreign country.

My mind went back to my college years at Andrews University in Michigan. I wasn't exactly sure what career to pursue, but I knew I wanted to work with kids, so I thought that maybe I'd be a child psychologist. I started off in psychology and ended up with a degree in behavioral sciences. In the meantime, my dad had urged me to take a minor in religion. "You never know, son, when it might come in handy," he'd tell me. "Who knows, you might become a pastor someday." I would laugh a bit, for I had about as much speaking ability and pastoral charisma as a rock. I was very shy, and would much rather stay home and read a book unless something fun like a basketball game was starting with my buddies.

"Me, a pastor?" I'd ask myself. Not on your life. In fact, not in a million years! I wasn't the right material to be a pastor. On the other hand, I couldn't figure out what other minor I wanted to take, so I did decide to take religion. Besides that, my dad had been known to be right on many other occasions. Little did I realize—until much later in life—how much the Holy Spirit used my dad to press me toward that religion minor.

During the teen years many young people think they know what they need and that they have the wisdom to make their own decisions. If you're a teenager, let me assure you of a well-known fact. Whether you will ever admit it or not, parents know a lot more about life and making wise decisions than you do right now. If you're a teen or even in your early 20s, do yourself a favor and listen to your parents. Most of the time you can't go wrong. God knew what He was talking about when He inspired Solomon with these words of vital importance: "Hear, my son, your father's instruction, and reject not your mother's teaching; for they are a fair garland for your head, and pendants for your neck" (Proverbs 1:8, 9, RSV). In other words: "Teens, listen to your parents, and I guarantee your life will be so much happier and so much easier than you would have ever dreamed possible." Unfortunately, though, we all know there are exceptions to the rule.

After graduation I went back to school and got a degree in elementary education, teaching school for the next five years. It was during this time, of course, that I lost my mother. In spite of this tragedy there was no question that I had a great experience working with kids. As I taught day . . . after day . . . after day, one thing kept coming to the forefront of my mind, and that was that I really enjoyed teaching the Bible classes. I wished that I could just teach Bible and skip the rest. But I don't suppose my students would have become well-rounded citizens if that's all they had learned from me, not to mention that I might have had some hotheaded parents breaking down my door. So I reluctantly kept teaching reading, writing, arithmetic, and all the rest, as well as Bible.

It was during my fifth year of teaching that God began to implant a very odd thought in my mind. I felt a call to the ministry. I had to ask the good Lord a number of times if He was sure He had the right man for the job. But the thought just wouldn't go away. In fact, it grew stronger and stronger by the day. In my mind I could hear my dad's words: *You never know, son. You might become a pastor someday.*

After a lot of prayer I finally decided that God was indeed leading my wife and me to the ministry. So we sent some résumés to a few Midwestern conferences, and sure enough, God opened a door in Marion, Indiana.

Quite frankly, I was scared to death of being a pastor. It didn't help my cause that I didn't have a Master of Divinity degree. I remember during the interview at Marion, one of the church elders, Palmer Smith, asked me, in front of everyone, who was going to help him with Greek. The only things *I* knew about Greek were that I could spell it in English and there was a broadcaster on TV named Jimmy the Greek. I stuttered and stammered something about my willingness to learn it. *Uh-huh, OK, yeah right, whatever. Learn Greek? Maybe a thousand years from now!*

I remember preparing for my first sermon not too long after that interview. I did more praying than actual writing my notes, which I've come to know is the best method. Not that a minister shouldn't aptly prepare. It's just that a lot of prayer needs to go into the preparation of every sermon. That first Sabbath morning, while sitting on the rostrum waiting to speak, I remember pleading with God to melt me into a little puddle and let me disappear through the cracks in the floor. I prayed this for two reasons. The first was so that the congregation would hear God, instead of me, speaking to them, and the other was so that the people wouldn't be able to hear my shaky voice and see my knees knocking together. Thinking back, I have no clue what the sermon was about, but when it was all over I was still standing and able to walk out of the sanctuary. I knew the Holy Spirit not only picked me up and carried me through that first sermon but also made me into a little puddle, and I was able to slip through the cracks in the floor and disappear!

I think it took me about a week to recover from my stress but I knew that from that point on this was God's ball game and I had absolutely nothing to do with any success that would come through my ministry. As long as I remained humble and teachable, constantly depending upon God through the power of prayer, God could use me to teach others.

Even today, every once in a while when I stand up to give a sermon I forget that God is speaking and I try to stand up with Him and put in my two cents' worth (all right, even two cents is stretching it a bit) with His pure gold. I have never left the sanctuary feeling good in my heart when I have forgotten to ask God to turn me into that little puddle and allow me to disappear into the cracks.

Sometimes I still wonder why in the world God asked me to be a pastor. I often feel like a little 5-year-old child trying to do a man's job. During those times God brings two scriptures to mind: "For when I am weak, then I am strong" (2 Corinthians 12:10) and "'Not by might, nor by power, but by My Spirit,' says the Lord of hosts" (Zechariah 4:6). Ellen White reiterates the same point in *Gospel Workers*. "When we have a realization of our weakness, we learn to depend on a power not inherent"(p. 509). You see, it's God doing the work. All of it. As long as I remember that I am the paintbrush and He is the Master Artist, then the spiritual windows of heaven are opened wide.

God has many ways to remind me that I am *only* the paintbrush, much loved but nonetheless still the paintbrush. Whenever I forget that vital piece of information, He lets me have it my way for a bit of time. He sits me down and lets me try to paint by myself. As you might figure, a paintbrush is completely worthless if left near the canvas by itself. It can't move; it can't mix the colors; it can't think about what it wants to paint; it can't even manage one brushstroke. It has no imagination, and it certainly can't come up with a masterpiece! So it usually doesn't take me long to realize that I need to be in the Master's hand for a Leonardo-like spiritual painting to come forth. It doesn't take a rocket scientist to figure this out. When was the last time you were in Paris and saw a crowd of people soaking in a beautiful piece of artwork and heard someone exclaim, "Man, what a paintbrush!" or "Wow, I'd sure like to meet the paintbrush that painted that masterpiece"?

So whether you're giving a sermon, typing a letter for the boss, or making supper for your family, never forget that you are a much-loved *helpless* instrument in the hands of a Father who will make you a complete success. Give Him all the credit and the glory. Remember that wise man who once said, "Before honor is humility" (Proverbs 15:33). Humble your little instrument self, and then He will lift you up and use you to share Jesus with those around you.

My family and I remained in Marion for three years. As can be expected, we found both trials and blessings all along the way. Quite honestly, I was far from being the kind of pastor I thought I should be. I made mistakes here and there, but for some reason God hung in there with me. I figure that God knows what we often won't grasp in a lifetime—what we're capable of in His hands.

It was during the middle of that third year that I began to hear that still small voice speak to my heart again. This time it wasn't a change of career, but a change of direction in my career. Earlier in the book I stated that ever since I was young, I felt that I wanted to work with kids in some form or fashion. Well, my early-childhood impression began to take shape in my mind, albeit a little differently than I had anticipated. It was as if God were asking me, "What would you say about a career in youth ministry?"

Work with teens? I'd much rather jump from the top of the Empire State Building without a parachute! The very thought caused the hair to stand up on the back of my neck and my legs to turn to something like blackberry jelly that's been cooking on the stove for an hour.

I have to be honest with you. When God impressed me to enter the youth ministry, I was afraid of teenagers. I knew what teenagers were like. I used to be a teenager, and *I* was scary! Teenagers know *everything*. They don't listen when you try to tell them something. You never know when they are telling you the truth or covering up with a lie. Teenagers don't want to hear about religion or spirituality. Teenagers want to be left alone with their friends. Teens are sneaky. Their worst characteristic is that they can see right through adults—and at that point in my life *I was an adult.*

Maybe I could try to meet God halfway. "Lord, how about if I work with *young* teenagers—say, second or third graders?" I asked. "Then at least I can still get the last word in if we get into any arguments about religion."

I'm telling you that every time I thought about the possibility of working with teens I started to sweat. My blood pressure leaped to about 200 over 120; my arteries started hardening up, too! It felt as if my shirts were squeezing my neck, and I couldn't breathe very well. "God, I'm going to need some help here. I'm scared, to put it bluntly. I don't think I'm even capable of handling teenagers. I know You will be with me and all that, but trust me, I can't do this. Could You give me some sign or some type of encouragement to lift the heavy burden I'm feeling? Fire from heaven would be good. Or maybe I could grow a foot taller overnight?"

At that point in my life I think that I felt a little like Gideon did when he was faced with leading a very small army against thousands and thousands of enemy forces. In fact, I would rather have been in Gideon's shoes than my own, facing tens and tens of teenagers! I thought about setting the fleece outside overnight, but I didn't know any sheep personally that might let me temporarily borrow their coat. After reading up on biblical ways of finding God's will, I figured that drawing straws or casting lots might give me some indication, but I would probably end up cheating on the test. So I kept pondering the inevitable as I tried to follow my normal pastoral routine.

One thing that really helped push me toward working with youth was that a good friend, Mike Edge—who happened to be Indiana's youth director—asked me to be the pastor for teen camp for a week. I reluctantly—but not without some excitement—agreed to the challenge.

Again, I prayed and prayed and *prayed* in preparation for this monumental event.

I knew that week could change my life. I also knew that if I failed as teen camp pastor I would never ever become a youth pastor. As that inevitable Sunday crept closer, my stress rose higher. I was on my knees a lot, pleading for God to help me figure out what spiritual insights to share with those teens who, I figured, probably wouldn't listen to me anyway. As scared as I was, I felt God's presence during those times of prayer. I knew that He wouldn't turn His ear away from my pleas.

I wish that I'd had more faith in God's Word than I did. It is loaded with promises to fit every situation we encounter. For starters, I think of Isaiah 59:1, which tells me, "Behold, the Lord's hand is not shortened, that it cannot save, or his ear dull, that it cannot hear" (RSV). One of my all-time favorite verses of Scripture is Isaiah 41:10: "Fear not, for I am with you, be not dismayed, for I am your God; I will strengthen you, I will help you, I will uphold you with my victorious right hand" (RSV). Then how can one look for strength from God without thinking of Paul's unanswerable question in Romans 8:31: "What then shall we say to this? *If God is for us, who is against us?*" (RSV). I had enough proof "from whence cometh my help" (Psalm 121:1, KJV), if my faith was willing to accept it. But amazingly I remained what you could call a Doubting Curt.

Sunday came, and my family and I were at camp early so we could get settled in our cabin. Everything was fine until the teenagers started coming in for registration. They gathered in little knots, talking and laughing among themselves, and I hovered on the outskirts trying to smile at them a bit, politely nodding now and then. Finally I thought that I'd try to mingle a bit to break the ice (that I was the only one walking on). When I spotted a couple of tough-looking guys and nice young women talking together, I decided it was time to jump into deep water.

"Hey, guys, how's it going?" I said, or something such as that.

They turned and looked at me. I looked at them. Nobody said a word in response to my question, though their collective glare said "Who are you?" and "Leave us alone!" I immediately thought that surely no human being could be so cold and heartless as not to at least say hi when someone is being so nice and friendly. *Or could they?*

I started to slip beneath the waves, so to speak, desperately looking for some buoy of words to save me from drowning on my first attempt at swimming in this deep dark pool. My mind had gone blank. And so I kept smiling and gracefully trying to nod as I walked backwards until I was close enough to the side of the building that I could turn and run away and hide in a badger hole and not come out until these scary teens were long gone and the second and third graders arrived!

Great job, Curt! Way to make a grand opening with these teens! I thought to myself. Yet I decided not to give up, thanks to the good Lord, who picked me up and carried me for a while. That's the way it is with God. So often when things are going really, really bad, you may wonder where in the world God went when the going got tough. You can rest assured that though He may not be talking much, it's because He's using His energy to carry you through those muddy holes in your life. You know, parents are a lot like God in this way. How many times, when you were 3 or 4 years of age and taking a hike with Mom and Dad, did you get completely worn out and feel as if your legs were going to quit if you took another step? How many times did your dad see your physical distress and quickly swing you up onto his shoulders, or how often did Mom gather you up into her arms and lovingly carry you the rest of the way home? Don't ever forget that God never gives you more than you can handle with Him, no matter how impossible it may seem.

I'm happy to say that by the end of that week I was talking to the teens and getting to know them. The good Lord actually used me to challenge their thinking and to guide some of them spiritually. The following Sunday at the week's end, I was walking on cloud nine. I thanked God so much for the strength He gave me and especially that He didn't allow me to quit when I was ready to leave. I can't say that I relaxed much that week, but I found out an important lesson. When dealing with teenagers, be yourself. Don't try to be someone or something that you aren't. Adults have to realize that they're not "one of the guys" anymore. Be an adult, and leave the being a teen to the teenagers. You'll get much more respect.

After that week at camp I felt a real push by the Lord toward youth ministry, but I wasn't in any hurry to make the change. We were nearing the three-year mark in Marion and I began to mentally sort out this whole idea of my working with teens. I felt so thankful for my wife at this point, because I needed someone to hear me verbalize my thoughts and concerns. Not only was Kim a good listener; she encouraged me to trust the Lord and to move out of my comfort zone. Her personality is always up for a new challenge! On the other hand, I could happily stay in one place my entire life. Blame it on my personality. Or blame it on a narrow-minded way of believing that wherever I was was the most important place in the world. The fact remains—I did not like change.

It was then that God decided I needed a kick in the pants. He knew that the time had come for me to venture out into the scary realm of teens. It happened as the family and I drove from Marion to Berrien Springs, Michigan, to see Kim's parents.

As the miles went by I was talking to Kim about whether or not we should move toward the youth ministry. I was just sharing my thoughts, but somehow it seemed that the Holy Spirit opened up my mind more than ever before as the story of David and Goliath powered its way into my thoughts. I shared with Kim my insights that the story of David and the giant had many similarities to working with youth. The more I talked, the more excited I got. It became crystal clear that God wanted me to work with young people. I knew these thoughts weren't my own.

Up to that moment I had never thought about any of the things that suddenly filled my view. For example, like Israel of old, here we sit asleep—the Laodicean church. Still God's people, but not doing much to usher in the second coming of Jesus. We're facing that Goliath who is making a mockery of our church, only today his name is Satan and his soldiers are the things of this world. Church leaders know we must push forward and fight this giant spiritual enemy, but few of us step out to lead. Like Israel of old, we're content to keep doing things as we always have, and to keep using the same old armor that worked in times past. Even so, during the time of David, God didn't forsake His chosen people, and God will not forsake us today. He sees that we are in a spiritual bind, and He has already planned ahead for it.

Thousands of years ago God searched until He found a youth who had a good relationship with Him, a youth who, when called to the forefront of the battle, would go "not by might nor by power, but by My Spirit" (Zechariah 4:6). It struck me on that eye-opening day that just as God needed David so long ago, today God needs men and women who are willing to do things differently from the way things have always been done before. He needs youth—many youth. That day in the car I suddenly knew that God was looking for youth to lead the way to victory, and He wanted me to get involved in the process!

By the time I finished sharing these thoughts with my wife we were almost to my in-laws' home. I was on fire and knew that God had called me to work with those dreaded teens! Little did I know that God wasn't quite finished with me. He knew that there was still about 10 percent of me that doubted even yet.

I praise God for His patience. As the Bible says in Psalm 103:14: "For He knows our frame; He remembers that we are dust." I was (and am) truly one of the dustiest human beings the world has ever seen.

But God is so patient with us and so forgiving when we don't trust Him to strengthen us as we face decisions. I thank God that He hung in there so long with me. Remember that when God called Moses, one of the greatest men ever to walk the earth, to do a work for Him, Moses pushed God's patience to the limit. Granted, Moses' calling was leaps and bounds ahead of mine, but still whether you are a Moses, a Joe, Mary, Ashley, or Curt, all of us struggle with the same tendencies to trust in ourselves and forget Him "who has made man's mouth" (Exodus 4:11).

It was about two weeks later that the final nail was hammered into this doubting coffin. Kim's parents came down to Marion to visit us one Sabbath afternoon. When they got there, I sat down with Norman, and we started some small talk. He asked me if I remembered Dave Ferguson, and I said that I did. Dave had been a good friend of mine while I attended Andrews University. Norman told me that Dave had had the Week of Spiritual Emphasis at Andrews and that he'd done a good job with his presentations. Then he started telling me about the sermon that Dave had given that very Sabbath morning. It was on David and Goliath! I sat spellbound listening to my father-in-law share almost exactly the same things that the Holy Spirit had brought to my mind two weeks before.

By the time Norman finished sharing the thoughts in Dave's sermon he was looking at me kind of funny. It was probably because my bottom jaw hung to the floor, causing me to drool all over the carpet. I tried to explain the shocked look on my face, but I figured he wouldn't believe that I'd had the same sermon come into my mind as I drove a car two weeks before. I figured that God had given me that amazing tap on the shoulder, and it wouldn't mean much to anyone else even if I tried to explain it. What had made this so special to me, even more than the sermon, was that Dave was in youth ministry—a conference youth director at the time. With this experience I knew that God wanted me to join Dave and numerous others who work with teens. I knew that God wanted me to lead young people to Him so He could find—as had young David of old—that perfect heart ready to help His people in their time of need.

One thing led to another, and it wasn't long after that David-and-Goliath revelation that my family and I were on our way to Maxwell Adventist Academy near Nairobi, Kenya. It was a long trip, and I was a little nervous as we neared Kenyatta Airport, then hung for a moment above the runway. Now, I have to be honest with you—I was *quite* nervous, and if I wasn't a man I would tell you that I was scared, but, of course, men aren't supposed to be afraid, so let's just say that I was mentally and emotionally challenged. How I prayed for God to help us. I told Him that I didn't really want to be there at all.

You see, I was the kind of kid who never left home except to sleep at Grandpa and Grandma's house once in a great while. I always thought that the whole world was Holly, Michigan. Before this trip I'd been out of the country on only two occasions—once to Mexico for a half day and then to Europe on a two-week vacation with my wife. Both trips caused me some serious high blood pressure. Believe me, the African continent was not my neck of the woods, and more than once on that second nine-hour flight I pondered holding a plastic butter knife to the necks of the pilots and forcing them to take me back home to America.

Then the wheels touched down and we glided to a stop. "I can't believe we're in Africa!" I said to myself. Who would have thought it possible that my family and I would be in Africa as missionaries? This must be a dream . . . or more likely a bad, bad nightmare. We stood up, gathered our carry-ons, and started leaving the plane. I was comforted some because my wife's cousin Terry Pottle and his family were flying with us. They had already been living at Maxwell for more than two years. We neared the gate, and I pushed my money way down in my pocket. We were heading into a big city, and I'm a small-city guy. Would someone try to lift my wallet or grab my carry-on and run? I kept my eyes opened wide and looking front, side, and behind me as if my life depended upon it. I wouldn't give up anything without a fight, Africa or not! I think I still remembered some tae kwon do from college and I wasn't afraid to use it!

As we walked through the corridor into the airport we saw some men holding a sign that said *DeWitts*. That was strange. Who in Kenya knew we were coming? We stopped short, eyeballing them suspiciously, and even Terry thought maybe someone was trying to pull a fast one on us. He asked them a couple of questions. They told him that they were there to meet the DeWitt family and that the DeWitts were supposed to come with them. What would they want with us? We'd just gotten there, and we hadn't had time to commit any crimes or anything. I couldn't tell from first glance if they were undercover policemen or what! I looked to Terry to take the lead, figuring he knew all there was to know about Kenya, and sure enough, he said that we should go on and walk down to the luggage area by ourselves. So we left the men holding up that sign, still looking for the DeWitt family. Hey, maybe there was another family named DeWitt coming off the plane. We did just fly in from Amsterdam, right? DeWitt is quite a common Dutch name, you know.

If only we'd known that those men were part of the airport police and that they'd been sent to help us get through baggage claim.

If we'd gone with them, our entrance into Kenya would have been so much more pleasant. A good friend of my in-laws, Esther Omoi (who with her family were missionaries in Kenya some years before), was closely related to the senior chief of the airport police. They had arranged for some officers to meet us and make sure we didn't encounter any problems on the way out. What a blessing would have been ours, and how much less hassle we would have had, if only we had trusted that God was looking out for us.

To me, this experience is similar to the Jacob and Esau story. Meeting Esau again after more than 20 years, Jacob feared for his life at the hand of his brother and prayed to God for help. Then when God laid His hand on Jacob's shoulder to offer comfort and help, Jacob assumed the worst and fought tooth and nail, taking matters into his own hands. If *I* hadn't been so busy worrying about all the things that could go wrong as I left my comfort zone and entered an unfamiliar country, I might have recognized the Holy Spirit's tap on the shoulder. I could have fallen safely in the arms of Jesus. I could have felt the perfect peace that comes because my mind was filled with trust in Him (see Isaiah 26:3). Instead, we turned the help and the blessing away.

Having a trusting relationship with God is really a very simple, easy-to-maintain process. It's only when we decide to muddy the water and do things *our* way or take things into *our* own hands that the trust part of that relationship goes awry and things begin to fall apart. But as I stated before, we humans are nothing but dust, while God is perfection and ultimate love. You know something, though? The best part is that He already knows that and amazingly still loves you and me no matter how many times we fail. Jesus died for you and me because even in our sinful state we mean the world to Him.

Don't ever allow Satan to convince you that you are unloved, unimportant, and worthless. If that were true, then Jesus would not have come to earth and died—just for you. But He did. God loves you so much that without hesitation He laid aside His divinity so He could feel what you feel, live the way you live, go through struggles and temptations like your struggles and temptations, and at last die for you so that you may come live with Him. The bottom line is that Jesus lovingly refused to let you go.

It was night when we arrived in Kenya. After some hassles with the exit security concerning what we had in our luggage and wanting to charge us for it, we gathered up Brindi and Smokey, our dog and cat who had traveled with us, and headed out to the school bus. Maxwell Adventist Academy, here we come! All the staff members had come to the airport to greet us, which was a nice blessing. They all seemed friendly enough, and I felt better than I had on the whole journey, albeit a bit tired out and not up for much conversation on the way to Maxwell.

It seemed that we rode for another two hours. Narrow streets. Bump after bump after bump. I'd later discover that from airport to campus was only a 45-minute ride, but that first time seemed much longer. At last we pulled into the driveway of what would be our home for the next year or so. It was quite an experience getting there, but more about that in the next chapter. Wearily we got out of the bus and trudged to the front door with our dog in the lead, sniffing around at all the new scents. Suddenly a huge dog came around the vehicle and up to Brindi. Actually, let me rephrase that. This dog went and stood over Brindi and had to get his binoculars out to see down to where her little puzzled face looked at him. This was the biggest dog I had ever seen. Besides that, he looked quite hungry, and I knew he'd have no trouble swallowing our cocker spaniel in one gulp without so much as a burp afterward.

Delamere, a beautiful German shepherd, looked like he'd listened to his mom when he was a pup and had eaten all his spinach. In fact, he was so big he looked like he ate everyone else's spinach too. At first glance I figured that he was either a descendant of Paul Bunyan's pet ox, he'd had a horse for a father, or he was from Texas. I quickly mumbled something about our dog being OK, and I remember seeing David Forsey calmly smile at me and say that I didn't have to worry.

Delamere was an amazing dog, and few in the world would match his loyalty to his owner. David was allergic to beestings, and more than once I saw Delamere, without being prompted, attack a bee that happened to fly too close to David. He'd grab it in his mouth and kill it, often getting stung in the process. I was deeply saddened when he had to be put to sleep because of some physical problems. I know it must have torn the hearts of David and his family. I will never forget that dog.

Everyone soon left us to ourselves, and we went into this house that had a metal ceiling and roof. Relieved that the long flights were finally over, we tried our best to settle into our beds, and finally went to sleep. We slept quite soundly that first night. In fact, the next thing I remember is hearing an owl hoot right over our heads on the roof. I leaped out of bed, waking my wife in the process, and told her that there was an owl on our roof. Over the past several years we'd enjoyed birding, and I had heard that there were lots of different species in Kenya. Kim joined me as we quietly opened the door and carefully peered on the roof. Much to our chagrin, there stood a speckled pigeon looking sideways at us as if we'd just lost our minds. So it wasn't the coveted owl, but it didn't matter to me.

After laughing at ourselves for five minutes, I stared around at the thorned acacia trees, banana palms, and distant hills. Looking down the hill a ways, I saw Kenyans walking by on a footpath. "I can't believe I'm in Africa!" I said to myself as I waved to the people, who waved back. This was great. In the States, I pondered, if you wave at someone they probably figure you want something or are giving them a nasty sign, and you might end up being shot. Here the people actually waved back and smiled.

You know, even after I lived there a whole year, the thought would hit me again: *I can't believe I'm in Africa!* I would start smiling, and that smile would stay on my face for the rest of the day. What a privilege to serve the good Lord in Kenya. I am so thankful that we went to Maxwell. God was in control through the whole process, and He is still in control today. What He taught me in Kenya proved to be so vital to my spiritual life that I wouldn't trade those six years for the world. I found that God is good all the time, and no matter what happens He is still in control. I can trust His ways even when I don't always understand everything.

When you are facing a lifetime decision or maybe just trying to figure out whether you should take a new job or perhaps move back in with Mom and Dad because you've run out of money, talk to God about it. See what His plan is, and remember that He has promised to take care of everything. It just requires some faith and a lot of patience on your part, because God works on His own timetable. He knows what will work best for you and everyone else involved. He can be completely trustworthy, because He has already watched your life movie and He knows exactly what to do and when to do it in order to bring about that storybook ending.

Remember, God is all-powerful, all-knowing, and all-everywhere. He is using *all His power* to save you! He knows *exactly* what you need in your life. He is as intimately involved in your life as though there weren't another person on the face of this planet. He is *always with you* every step of the way—through your good and your bad times. How can you go wrong by surrendering your life completely to Him? You can't.

Chapter 3

Driving on the
Wrong Side of the Road

*Walk through the narrow entrance that leads to Christ. The way that leads
to heartache, sorrow, and eternal death is a huge, easy-to-follow road, and nearly
everyone in this world is traveling on it. But the other way is a tremendously narrow
path and, at times, very difficult to follow, which is why most people travel the easier
way. But if you travel this narrow way, you will have a constant Companion who
will lead you to Jesus, perfect peace, and eternal life! (Matthew 7:13, 14, PCRV).*

I 'll not soon forget the first time I rode in a vehicle that was
traveling on the wrong side of the road. (It was the wrong
side of the road only because I had an American mind-set that
had turned to cement over the past 34 years of my life.) It was that
first bus ride from the airport to Maxwell Academy. The bus was
fairly full of people, and I was sitting four or five seats from the
front. As we took off, one frightening thing was foremost in my
mind. David Forsey was doing an awful lot of looking around
even as he drove down the road. I was positive that we were
going to be killed and I wouldn't have experienced even one
night's sleep in Kenya.

I have ridden with some really bad drivers, people who simply
couldn't do two things at once. It is impossible for some people to
keep up a conversation and drive at the same time. Once I rode with
a driver whose hands were attached to his eyeballs. Every time he
looked over at me in the passenger seat his hands came too, to see
what the conversation was all about. I wouldn't normally have any

41

difficulty with that except that the hands brought their close friend the steering wheel with them, and we all got a close-up of a beautiful tall maple tree standing near the road! Needless to say, I did my best *not* to ride with that person again.

This first trip to Maxwell took the cake, however. I was amazed that Bert Williams, the pastor and music teacher, didn't appear to be bothered at all by David's driving, even though he was in the front passenger seat. Everyone was talking and having a good time . . . everyone except me! To make matters even worse, Lloyd Dull, the science teacher, was trying to break into the *Guinness Book of World Records* by seeing how many Kenyan horror stories he could tell the newcomers during one 45-minute trip! But David was simply unbelievable. Quite a number of times he *actually* turned completely around, facing the back of his seat, talking and laughing with me and others. *Great,* I thought, as I tried hard to swallow my heart, which had leaped into my throat. *We survived the 17 hours of flying and the scary arrival at the airport, only to be killed because a bus driver didn't listen to rule number two during driver's education class: Always keep your eyes on the road.* The first rule, of course, was *Always fasten your seat belt.* Believe me, I not only had my seat belt securely fastened but was also trying to undo the two seat belts next to my seat so I could fasten those around me too. If we were going down, I wasn't going without a fight.

I know you may find this difficult to believe, but somehow David was able to keep the bus on the road and we didn't even come close to hitting any trees, cars, or buildings on the way to Maxwell. This guy defied all logic. I've always heard that elementary teachers have eyes in the back of their heads, but I knew that was just a saying. It wasn't true or even physically possible, so I figured that this was a miracle. Surely even God must have had an incredulous look on His face as He witnessed David's *skilled* driving. It's entirely possible, I pondered, that God figured it wouldn't do much to encourage other missionaries to come to Kenya if they read in the *Headline News* that a whole campus had been killed because of bad driving, so maybe He sent His angels to steer the wheels.

At this point I looked over at my wife. I figured that she'd have her head bowed and be praying for all she was worth. This situation seemed strangely familiar to me as I recalled the one time we traveled by taxi through a city in Italy. Throughout the entire trip Kim and I sat in the middle of the back seat, praying and holding each other as tightly as possible. The taxi driver raced back and forth, switching lanes as if he were driving in the Indy 500! He even drove on the sidewalk a couple times, and laid on the horn the whole trip. The Italian taxi drivers have no respect for anyone, not even the police. Curse the police car who happened to be in *his* way! We raced up behind one police car, and our driver laid on the horn. When the car didn't pull over, the taxi passed on the sidewalk, and the officer acted as though he didn't even see us. Let me give you a small piece of advice. If you get stressed while driving on your own or with someone else, trust me, don't ever live in Italy!

So I looked over at Kim and saw a calm, serene look on her face. I figured she wasn't paying careful attention, so I quietly enlightened her so I wouldn't offend David. "Hey, do you see the way he's driving?" I whispered. "He turns around every time somebody talks to him. We're going to *die!*" Kim looked at me to see if I was serious and then said with a grin on her face and a laugh in her voice, "Hon, he's not driving. The steering wheel is on the other side of the vehicle."

Pastor Williams had been driving the bus the whole time.

Boy, talk about being overwhelmed with relief. I was so happy, and since a couple of the staff had overheard part of our conversation, I laughed and said, "Man, I was pretty worried because David kept looking around. I was getting nervous. I thought he was driving the bus this whole time!"

David turned all the way around in his seat one more time and laughed heartily. I was lucky that I had a good excuse to cover my ignorance. "Wow! That was one long flight over here," I laughed. "I must be really tired and partially brain-dead." I don't think any of the staff bought it, but it was worth a try.

We were driving down Mombasa Road, a divided two-lane highway, during all this. It seemed a bit weird to look out the window and see car headlights to my right instead of left, but I didn't think much of it until the highway ended and we began a trek with cars coming straight at us on a regular one-lane road. The feeling I experienced was definitely not pleasant. My point of reference was opposite to the current reality. Seeing bright glaring headlights coming toward us from the right side of the road—a for-sure head-on collision—was enough for me to hang up my missionary shoes forever. And after seeing a few vehicles pass us on the "wrong" side of the road, I decided that it was best to stop looking out of the window and do something more beneficial—like pray!

Praise the Lord, we made it home safely and were quite happy to be off that monster road. By this time gray hair had started to sprout on my head, and I figured that if this was any indication of what we could expect for the future, by the time our six years were up I'd look like an old grandpa.

I knew that sooner or later I would have to drive on the "wrong" side of the road too. I felt pretty excited about the opportunity, and little did I realize how dangerous it is for the first few months of doing so. It's a bit difficult to take 19 years of driving on the right-hand side of the road and suddenly start driving on the left. I compare it to starting to walk backward instead of forward or eating with your left hand when you've used your right all your life.

My first time sitting in the "wrong" side of the car, driving down the "wrong" side of the road wasn't as bad as I figured it would be. Once on the road, staying in my lane was not a problem. The dangerous part came when I had to make a turn and go in another direction. The normal thing to do when you need to turn right is just to do it. In the States, when you turn to the right you don't cross traffic. But in Kenya, even though my mind said to turn without another thought, I was going to cross traffic and might end up another road statistic if I turned without first looking. That first three months it was a constant battle to think carefully while I drove. I recall at least a half dozen times that I actually turned without thinking and could have been in an accident. God was ever my protector, and I know He had a wonderful hand in protecting us during those times.

After we went back to the U.S. for the first of our two furloughs, I had quite a time trying to stay on the right side of the road, so to speak. A couple of times I found myself driving down the oncoming lane of traffic oblivious to the world. Each time I quickly adjusted, checking my rearview mirror to see if any friendly neighborhood police cars were coming to give me a breathalizer test and take my license away for three months. On the second furlough, driving on the right side of the road was twice as hard as the first. I had become a Kenyan driver whether I liked it or not, and the sooner we got back to Kenya the safer we would be!

Let me take the opportunity to tell you what kind of road laws they have in Kenya. The main law is this: If you get to the open spot on the road first, it's yours. What exactly does this mean? You're sitting on a side road waiting to turn onto a main road. You look down the road the opposite way you are heading, and you see a *matatu* (minivan taxi) coming at 75 miles (120 kilometers) per hour. The van is only about 50 feet (15 meters) away, but you notice that there's plenty of space for you to pull into regardless of the fast-approaching *matatu*. So you follow the rule of the road and swiftly pull out. Simply put, that space in the road is yours. The *matatu* has three choices: quickly pass you, slam on the brakes to avoid your bumper, or run off the road and take out two thorn trees in the process. But no matter his choice, he won't do the American thing and pull out a bazooka and blow you away out of road rage. At most, he may pass you and hold his open hand out the window with palm up and bent at the wrist, which basically means, "Maybe you should have waited till I passed you. What do you think? But if you don't agree with me on this matter, then *hacuna matata!* [no problems, no worries]."

I kid you not. You will hardly ever hear a horn honk unless it's because someone is passing you on a narrow road, and then only because they want to let you know they are coming so you don't move over too far. The other times you hear horns honking are the times the *matatus* are trying to get waiting passengers' attention to see if they want a ride. The horns make the most unusual sound I have ever heard. If you couldn't see, you would swear, after hearing the horns for about an hour at a usual pickup spot, that Kenya is full of tugboats and trains. *Matatu* drivers have the distinction of always choosing to lay on their horns exactly when you are passing by with your window wide open. Sometimes just for fun I'd wait with my hand on my own horn and lay it on thick just as a *matatu* passed me by. It gave me a little satisfaction once in a while even though it wasn't a very nice thing to do. I figure they must go to *matatu* school and practice this precise timing of horn honking. Maybe when they nail 100 cars in a row they graduate. I don't know. But it's no co-incidence that I'm now mildly deaf in my right ear.

I must admit that even after living in Kenya for six years, I still haven't completely conquered the road rage or what I like to call "road a-little-bit-angry" mentality. I've come a long way, but 19 years is too long to change overnight. The funny thing is that if you do happen to see an angry driver in Kenya discreetly using the middle finger or shouting curses at another driver, it typically ends up being an American, a European, or a young guy from India. We could learn so much from Kenyan people, but I'll share more about them in a later chapter.

Matatus can be quite a nuisance if you are following directly behind one with no ample opportunity to pass. The horn honks, the *matatu* stops, usually right in the middle of the road, picks up a passenger or two, and pulls out, repeating the process many times before you finally can get around it. One day we were following a *matatu* with two guys hanging out the sliding door as it raced down a hill. Nearing the bottom, the van began to slow, and the guys ducked inside. In the same moment the van's sliding door started a forward slide at a tremendous speed. Imagine our surprise when the van came to an abrupt stop and the door slid right past its usual stopping point and kept right on going. We were thankful that there were no bystanders in that place, for they surely would have been injured or worse. We stopped and watched, trying to keep our sides from splitting, as the men got off and trekked up to the temperamental door, carried it back to the vehicle, and reattached it. They then continued on their merry way as if it were nothing out of the ordinary. On the other hand, I admire the matter-of-fact way in which they dealt with the problem.

If you want to see something unusual, then you must come to Kenya, for as I said, anything that can happen will happen here. On another day we were headed home from the supermarket when we came around a corner and, to our shock and dismay, saw about 10 cow heads scattered across the road. Surprisingly, each was upright, and they were all staring directly at us, eyes wide open. A truck had rounded the corner too fast and overturned. It just so happened to be carrying cow's heads in the back. What memories Kenya has given us! We couldn't forget them even if we tried.

What really makes driving in Kenya special is the condition of the roads. Where do I begin when writing about the roads? Let me try to drum up a word that summarizes these roads: ummmm—ah—kind of like, um— You know what? I don't think there is any word in my vocabulary or in the English language (and definitely not in Swahili) that aptly fits the description of Kenyan roads. Let me give you a few synonyms, though, to get you as close to the real thing as possible—bad; terrible; terribly bad; really terribly bad; really badly terrible; really, really terribly badly terrible. Do you get the picture? They are simply terribadly!

When my dad first went to Kenya for a visit, I told him that since I'd gone there to live, I didn't seem to have many back problems anymore. After riding awhile on the roads he wasn't sure if I was telling the truth or not. But by the end of his safari he said, "You know, Curt, you were right. My back feels pretty good. My neck is killing me, but my back is better." We got quite a good laugh at that one.

Near the end of their vacation we took my dad and our good family friends Ingrid and Earl Kincaid with us to the Mombasa coast. Just before we came into town, we hit an area of the road with holes so large that our car nearly disappeared until it came out the other side—craters galore. At one point I decided that they shouldn't go home without really experiencing running over a big Kenyan bump or two. So I hit one squarely at quite a decent speed, and as I glanced at the back seat I saw that my dad had completely left his seat and hit his head on the ceiling, which was about two feet higher than his head. Three seconds later he came down to join the rest of us.

After living there for six years, I laugh at how the whole state of Michigan panics when there happens to be a hole on some major highway because somebody might get in an accident. I guarantee that I will never utter one complaint about bad roads in the States no matter how bad they may seem to everyone else.

What would African roads be like if you didn't see donkeys, cows, sheep, goats, or stray dogs in the middle of them? Quite often, even once in a while in Nairobi, it isn't unusual to see some animals in the middle of the road. The goats and the dogs are fairly smart. As you come closer they'll run off the road, and you usually don't even have to honk your horn. Sheep and cows, on the other hand, are quite lazy and quite lacking in intelligence. If sheep are in the road and you come close, they all just stand there and look around to see if anyone else is panicking. And when they see everyone else looking around, they all look as though they'd just lost their marbles, and then slowly mosey off the road. Most often they need a young Kenyan shepherd to fling a couple of rocks their direction for encouragement. But if they're on the side of the road, the last thing you want to do is honk your horn, because they'll most likely run directly in your path. I will not forget the time a sheep ran in front of our vehicle. Since I couldn't dash to the other lane because of oncoming traffic and couldn't stop in time, I hit the poor sheep. I felt very bad, as it struggled for about a minute before expiring.

Cows move even slower than sheep. They are docile as can be and not in a hurry *in the least!* You can pull up next to them and just lay on your horn. They'll look your direction, and if they are in the mood, they may amble off the road in their own good time. Sometimes I've been known to slowly pull our vehicle up to their posteriors and give them a little bump for good measure. For about two seconds the bump *slightly* increases their speed; then they seem to forget the trauma that just occurred.

Donkeys have somehow figured out how to speak Swahili. Not only do they understand what *hacuna matata* means, but they have mastered the art of having no worries or problems. Many times I have pulled up right next to a cluster of donkeys who are having a meeting in the middle of the road. With them directly in front of my bumper I've laid on the horn for two full minutes. They don't look at the car and don't even wiggle an ear! They simply don't care how long I honk my horn; they're *not* moving today, tomorrow, or any time in the near future.

When donkeys are blocking your way you can either go around or take a nap, and when *they* feel like moving they'll let you know. One thing I never tried was holding a tidbit in front of their noses to see if I could con them off the road. Come to think of it, I'm not even sure what a donkey eats or if it'd even care.

I'll not soon forget the day my wife and I saw what I like to term Revenge of the Humans! We were headed to town from Maxwell, and as we came up the big hill into the town of Ongata Rongai, we saw a sight to behold. Now, remember that donkeys are stubborn, and I had been irritated by their behavior numerous times. That's what made this so enjoyable. We saw a cart loaded with containers full of water that was attached to a very unfortunate donkey. The cart was so heavy that when the young driver attempted to get his donkey to pull it up onto the tarmac, the weight lifted the donkey off his hooves and suspended it about four feet off the ground.

Say I have a weird sense of humor, but I hadn't had that kind of hearty laugh take hold of my insides for a long time. It was simply hilarious to me. The donkey had an incredulous look on his face as it hung by its harness, swinging to and fro. I guess he figured that his lazy life was finally coming to an end. It was even funnier to see two guys also hanging on to the donkey, trying desperately to pull him back down to the pavement. I can't say that I felt *any* sorrow in the least for that poor donkey.

Of course, this particular donkey hadn't done me any harm. I supposed that he represented all the donkeys of Kenya to me, and all the time I'd spent trying to move them off the road.

So if you are ever driving on the roads of Kenya and you see dogs or goats on the road, slow down a bit, but keep moving.

They'll likely get out of your way before you get to them. If it's sheep or cows, then come to a complete stop. If they're doing their best to irritate you by not moving (as if they know you're late for picking up your pizza from a nearby restaurant), you can give them a little bump with your car. But if it is donkeys, just stop the car, turn off the key, and break out a picnic lunch with some Beethoven—you may be there for a while.

You know, I have learned a lot of spiritual lessons from driving the roads of Kenya. Whether you are one who hasn't ever followed Jesus or you think you've been on the right road spiritually speaking, maybe it's time to move out and try something new. God's way. Looking back over my earlier life, I remember driving my car of life down the easy roads much like those in the United States. It's so simple living within your comfort zone, not to mention that everyone else seems to be traveling the same direction and driving on the same side of the road.

Sometimes we humans get used to certain habits and particular ways of doing things, spiritually and otherwise. The regular spiritual roads seem smooth and relatively easy to maintain. But you know, God calls us all out of this world. In Revelation 18:4 we can hear the pleading voice of our Father in heaven: "Come out of her, my people, lest you take part in her sins" (RSV). God wants us to leave the comfort and safety of the way it has always been and come to Him. Become a pilgrim in this place and begin to walk the narrow way that leads away from this world toward life, instead of that broad road that leads to eternal loss.

Driving in country new to you (such as Kenya) is similar to traveling on God's narrow road. It won't be easy. There will be rough bumps along the way, not to mention the fact that you'll be going against traffic on the opposite side of the spiritual road. It will take some time to get used to walking with God on *His* side of the road. But after a time it becomes easier. You see, God is leading the journey, and you can let Him take care of everything. You'll still have those crater-sized temptations along the way, and yes, that animal, the roaring lion, stubborn Satan, will try to step in front of you and block your path to Jesus. But with patience God will take over the wheel and bump that stubborn animal right off the road. Soon you'll see the bright lights of Zion ahead.

Yes, it's a rough journey but you'll have a constant Companion by your side the whole time. He has been living on these roads a long time, and He knows exactly what will work and what will fail. Just sit in the passenger seat, fasten your seat belt, and get to know your Savior as you travel along the way. You will make it to the end of your spiritual journey feeling a peace and happiness you've never felt before. As Jesus tells us, "I am the way, the truth, and the life" (John 14:6) and "As one whom his mother comforts, so I will comfort you" (Isaiah 66:13).

Remember the words to that old hymn: "This world is not my home, I'm just a-passing through." It's heaven that's our home— that place where Jesus dwells, where He has a special home all prepared, just awaiting our arrival. Travel the strange, maybe unfamiliar, new road that leads to life, and by the end of time—or the end of your life, and maybe even before then—you will see that it was well worth it!

Chapter 4

Two Thieves Against
12 Prayer Warriors

I pray to You, my Lord. Don't fail me, for I am trusting You.
Cause my enemy to fail in his attempt to take advantage of my willingness to
help others. Make him ashamed for his actions that he may repent of his ways.
Help me wait patiently, knowing You will see my tears and bring justice to
my enemy mingled with mercy and forgiving love (Psalm 25:1-3, PCRV).

During our first year at Maxwell I decided to start a student prayer warriors group. My goal was to help the spirituality of both students and staff, drawing us even closer to God. This was based on something I'd read that really made an impact on me. "Prayer is the breath of the soul. It is the secret of spiritual power. . . . Prayer brings the heart into immediate contact with the Wellspring of life, and strengthens the sinew and muscle of the religious experience. Neglect the exercise of prayer, or engage in prayer spasmodically, now and then, as seems convenient, and you lose your hold on God" (Ellen White, *Messages to Young People,* pp. 249, 250). Truly prayer is needed in every organization and in each of our lives, so that we may grow spiritually and walk the narrow path that leads to life eternal.

So the prayer group began, meeting unobtrusively at my home on Friday evenings after vespers. If my memory serves me correctly, 12 young dedicated students quietly became a mighty tool for God at Maxwell Academy. Little did I know then how much I would need those prayer warriors later that year. I love how God always plans ahead for the crises we encounter. What a loving Father we have.

One day about a month after school started, I answered a knock at our door. There I found two smiling gentlemen who greeted me in the name of Jesus. I had never met them before, but for some reason they knew that I was a pastor. They say that even the rocks have ears in Kenya, and after six years there I just about believe it. As I returned their greeting I noticed that one of the men had a horrible scar across his face. It made me shudder as I listened patiently to his story. He had been riding in a *matatu* and had been thrown through the windshield. He was lucky to be alive. He kept praising God over and over that his life had been spared, and I felt drawn to this young man, who couldn't have been more than 30 years of age. He showed me a hospital bill of more than 150,000 Kenyan shillings, equivalent to more than US$2,000 at that time. That's a lot of money in Kenya. To give you a fair idea, any person working full-time earning the minimum wage would be fortunate to earn that amount in five or six years.

I felt very bad for this young man and willingly gave him about 1,000 shillings to help him with his bill. He was so appreciative. He thanked me profusely and praised God for blessing him. I prayed with the two men, and after they left I felt good inside that I had done a little to help someone in need.

It wasn't but a month later that I again received a visit from Michael and his good friend, who seemed to be his caretaker. Again he came to my door praising God for nearly everything he could think of, and thanking me for helping him. During this visit he showed me a prescription that the doctor had said he must purchase to help the healing process on his face. So I decided that he needed the help and I gave him some more money to help with the cost of the medicine. Again we prayed, and he was the most thankful person I had seen in a long time. I appreciated his pleasant attitude.

Just as he and his friend were about to leave, Michael turned to me and asked me if I'd be willing to help him with a difficulty. I asked him to share what it was, and so he told me about a friend of his in the States, a certain priest who had visited Kenya and had gotten to know Michael quite well. Michael said that his stateside friend was aware of the accident and had raised some funds through his church and wanted to help Michael pay his hospital bill.

I thought that was very nice of the priest to make such a grand effort, and I asked Michael how I could help him with this dilemma. He said that the priest wanted to make sure that the money got to the right person and was used for the right purpose. Would I be willing to cash the check that Michael would bring to me and then collect receipts from him so he could prove that he was spending it as the church had designated?

I thought about it and didn't figure that there would be any harm in this process. I would cash the check for him and give him the money. He would bring the receipts to me, and I would file them in a folder and eventually send a letter or an e-mail to the priest, letting him know the results. I wasn't about to be lied to, so I said that I would help him, but that I would require every shilling spent to be accounted for by receipt, with *no exceptions*.

"Oh, yes, Pastor, I will make sure I bring you receipts for all the money. I promise God as my witness to be honest if you will only help me," he graciously responded.

So I agreed with a handshake, and he told me that he would return in a couple of days with the first check, which had already been sent to him. As soon as he left, Kim came into the room. She had overheard everything. "Curt, don't do this. You don't know if he is honest or not. What if he doesn't return with the receipts?"

I retorted, "Well, if he doesn't return with the receipts, then the deal is off, and I won't cash any other checks the priest sends. I'm not out anything either way. He will be the loser if the priest has planned to send more money on a consistent basis."

"I wouldn't do it!" Kim told me. "You don't know some of the people here in Kenya. Just like anywhere else, not everyone is honest."

I laughed at her fears and told her that I would be careful and collect all the receipts and that everything would be OK, and besides, we should be doing our Christian duty and be helping others in need. She left, shaking her head, mumbling that I should do some more checking into his situation, so I decided to investigate a bit further. I had one of the hospital bills, so I called the hospital. I figured that if he was, in fact, lying to me I would find out, as the hospital would have records of any outstanding bill. After explaining that I wanted to help this man pay his bill, they checked in the computer and found that Michael was indeed a former patient and had a large bill of approximately the amount he had shared with me. So I hung up feeling very satisfied that he was telling me the truth. I was glad to carry through with my plans to help my brother. After I shared what I'd learned, my wife felt more satisfied about it too.

A few days later Michael brought the first check to me. It was for $1,000, or about 70,000 shillings. That was a lot of money. Michael was so happy and praised the Lord for His help. I told him to come back in about two days and I would give him the money, reminding him that I must have all the receipts from the total amount before I would cash the next check from the priest. He assured me that wasn't going to be a problem, and when he returned about a week later he had receipts that accounted for all of it. He had bought a bed and told me that he hadn't had anything to sleep on but the floor. One receipt was for the medicine and another was for necessary household items. I don't exactly recall getting a receipt from the hospital, but I think some amount was put on his bill.

The same day that he came with the receipts he brought another check for $2,000, which he readily handed over to me. We set a day later that week when he would come by for the money. A good friendship developed between us during this process. Sometimes we'd visit for up to a half hour, and we always prayed together before he left. He seemed to be one of the finest Christian gentlemen I'd ever met. I knew that God had a plan in mind for this young man, scars and all. It did my heart good to know that I was an instrument God was using to help one of His poor children. It was worth any trouble I went through, getting to town to cash the check and keeping records.

Michael was quite excited about the help I was giving him. Not only was he going to pay off his medical bill, but he'd received a letter from his friend saying that they wanted to help him go through school and get a degree. So the amounts of money were going to keep coming for a few months. I was very happy for him, as it is quite difficult for a Kenyan to afford even secondary school, let alone college. What an opportunity for Michael. What a blessing God was bestowing upon him during this traumatic time after the accident.

About two weeks later Michael arrived with the third check from the priest, this time for $4,000. This was huge, and I could sense that Michael had never seen so much money in his life. The approximately 280,000 shillings would be an unbelievable amount. When I first looked at the check, I thought, *Maybe it's not a good idea to give him this all at once. He could get robbed or something on his way home.* But I finally decided that I would cash it at the exchange bureau located not far from Maxwell.

The day before I planned to cash the $4,000 check I received a phone call from my friend at the exchange bureau. This call sent my life in a downward spiral—spiritually, emotionally, and mentally.

"Pastor DeWitt, there seems to be a problem with the $2,000 check you recently cashed," she told me. "It bounced, and was returned to us. It seems that the check was stolen from some tourists who came through Nairobi about a month ago. Could you please come to the exchange and take care of this?"

To say that I was stunned is to put it mildly. I am usually idealistic in my approach to human beings, and never in a thousand years would I have imagined that a person could lie and feign Christianity the way Michael did to me. I was speechless. It had never dawned on me that I might actually get stuck with paying back the amount of the checks out of my own pocket.

"How could this happen to me, Lord?" I prayed. "You know that I was innocently trying to help this man and his friend. How could I have been so blind and stupid at the same time? Lord, why didn't You impress upon me the evil intent of these two men?"

The more I thought about the situation, the sicker at heart I became. The $2,000 check had bounced, which meant that sooner or later the $1,000 check was also going to bounce. Our already-meager account would now shrink even further to the tune of $3,000. What would my wife say? How was I ever going to live this down? I talked to her about it, and she was as encouraging as possible, even though she too did not feel very good about what had transpired. I went to the exchange bureau and paid the money with a very heavy heart. My friend felt bad about it, but there was nothing she could do.

After I left the exchange, I began to experience a change in emotions. That natural revengeful spirit of humanity reared its ugly head. I wanted to kill this guy. No, not literally, but I wanted to give him a few good swings, which would make me feel a lot better inside. "Oh, yes," I begrudgingly told myself, "wouldn't that be a pretty headline on the local news station: 'Pastor of Seventh-day Adventist church at Maxwell Adventist Academy pummels local thief in revenge for ripping him off for $3,000! Report at 9:00!'"

Of course, I knew I couldn't go beat up this guy. That would dishonor God and my profession, not to mention my church. But what could I do? My mind churned with worry. If only I knew where he lived, I could take the police to his door and get my money back, but I didn't have a clue. Of course, he wouldn't let me in on that little detail.

But it wasn't too long before I discovered that I had a little green friend on my side that *could* turn the tide against Michael. This friend's name was greed! Michael had already benefited from the $3,000. Surely he wouldn't be satisfied with that when the possibility existed that he could get more. Yet for some odd reason he stopped coming by for visits, calling me instead about my cashing the $4,000 check. He seemed very nervous on the phone and asked whether or not I had the money, saying he could come get it. He told me that he wanted to enroll in college classes.

I didn't want to lie, because I believe that God wants us to tell the truth, no matter the circumstances, so I told him the truth. "Michael, come on by the house and I'll take care of everything," I said truthfully, figuring I'd be taking care of justice—not handing out money to these two thieves. I asked him when he wanted to come by so we could work this money thing out. He said that he'd call me again later that week. I had no choice but to wait for the next phone call.

During the following days I struggled between depression and anger. I was really down and out. I had difficulty keeping up my duties as a pastor. Even at home I walked around the house with my head hanging low. This situation went way beyond the loss of money. I had trusted people, and they had stabbed me in the back and stomped me into the ground. A light went out in my heart toward people, in particular Kenyans. The feeling scared me, because I felt that never again could I trust another soul, no matter how honest and upright they appeared. It felt very unnatural to me not to trust others. I didn't like it and felt that it went against being a Christian, against having that giving spirit that never wearied in well doing (see Galatians 6:9).

I felt my life spiraling out of control, and I didn't know how to counteract it. I prayed and prayed and prayed. I asked God for justice and begged Him to help me out of my pit of despair. And even though I didn't feel God's comforting hand at the time and even figured I was too self-absorbed for Him to hear me, He *did* hear my heartfelt cry. He knew that there was one way to lift me up, something I never considered. It never occurred to me that I needed the sympathy of fellow human beings with like passions and temptations.

Days passed with no phone calls from Michael. As the end of the week neared, Satan pressed me with temptations from all sides. I had called my dad earlier that week and received comfort from him as he prayed for me over the phone. But as another two days went by, I sunk deeper and deeper into self-pity until I was stuck fast. Deeply depressed, feeling like a failure, I was ready to quit being a pastor and to go back home to the States. My wife, bless her heart, saw that I was in dire straits and that this was a spiritual emergency. So after dark and without my knowledge, she called the student prayer warrior leader and asked if all the team could come over to the house and pray for me.

I recall sitting in the living room of that tin house feeling lost.

And as I sat there buried in my deeply sad thoughts, I heard a knock at the door. In came one of the prayer warriors and quietly sat down. A few moments later another arrived, and then still another, until the complete group of 12 prayer warriors sat quietly around the room sympathetically looking my way. Even though I preferred to be alone, I forced a smile. I figured that I knew why they were there, and even though I didn't think it would help, I would never turn them away. After all, I'd been trying to teach them that God hears and answers prayers and has the power to turn circumstances around.

They asked if we could all kneel in prayer together, and I half-heartedly agreed. I knelt down, and they surrounded me in a circle, joining hands and leaving me alone in the center. Then began the most touching prayers I had ever witnessed in my life. As I listened to these young spiritual leaders, a small light began to flicker in the depths of my soul. With each prayer that light burned brighter and brighter. I could sense that the Holy Spirit was present, and it was all because 12 young people were determined to move the right arm of God on my behalf. I wasn't used to being the one who needed to be prayed for. I was the pastor; I usually prayed for others.

Pastors often get the mind-set that their job is to pray for others, with no thought that they too need prayer. I've often felt that I must live the perfect life—always trusting in God, always having strong faith, always helping others, and never asking for help and support from anyone. A pastor's life is often a lonely lot. But how wrong it is for me to feel that way. I am human, just like everyone else. It is a fact that God holds pastors and church leaders to a higher standard, but we must never assume that pastors have everything figured out and that their lives are perfect. Nothing could be further from the truth. We all need Jesus each and every day, bar none! "For all have sinned and fall short of the glory of God" (Romans 3:23). Pastors have the same struggles as everyone else. In fact, their struggles are often intensified simply because they are spiritual leaders. Wherever you are, I plead with you to pray for your pastors. Lift them up to God every day. None of us can survive without your prayers and sympathies. Your pastors need you just as much as you need them.

My heart melted, and I felt the tears come as prayer after prayer lifted me higher and still higher into the loving arms of Jesus. Then came the last prayer from the Association of the Student Body spiritual vice president, Glauber. All the prayers were meaningful and meant the world to me, but Glauber's prayer—the last prayer—seemed to knife its way into the depths of my soul. It went something like this:

"Father, You know Pastor Curt's heart! You know he was trying to help these two men and had good intentions. Dear God, You can give him back that $2,000. Nothing is too hard for You. If it is Your will, give him that $2,000 and show Him that You are with him and will continue to guide him. . . .We lift him up to You, asking that You take care of everything and let him feel Your arms of love embracing him. Nothing is too hard for You, O God. . . ."

After Glauber finished praying, we all stood up. Tears filled my eyes. The Holy Spirit was in that room, and each of us felt His power. We knew that the God of the universe had just heard the cries of His children and had come to us in our home to comfort and pour out His love. As those 12 warriors hugged me and one another I knew that somehow everything was going to be all right. God was still in control of my life, and He had what it took to carry me out of that pit of despair. After they left, I hugged my wife and thanked her for calling them. Later I went to bed and fell into a good, peace-filled sleep, the first in a long time. It was that evening that Galatians 6:2 took on a new meaning in my life. "Bear one another's burdens, and so fulfill the law of Christ." My student brothers and sisters had come and placed their shoulders under my heavy burden and strengthened me.

The next morning, I awoke and began a new day—back with Jesus. I still felt the stinging loss of that $2,000 (which I knew would soon be $3,000). I felt pain every time I recalled the situation, but God was in control, and I tried desperately to hand that empty feeling to Him. Little did I know how *much* God was in control and that His plan of action was already in motion.

Around 8:00 p.m. two days later I heard the telephone ring one long tone instead of the usual two tones that indicated an on-campus call. The one long tone was the long-distance ring, which often meant that a family member was calling from the United States. I picked up the receiver and heard my dad's voice calling from Florida. "Curt, Curt, I've got some news to tell you!" he blurted.

My first thought was that someone in the family was either dying or had been killed. I held my breath, waiting to hear the worst.

"Curt, you aren't going to believe this, but after you told me about losing that $2,000, I felt so bad that Wednesday evening I shared it with our prayer meeting group. We had a special prayer for you. After the meeting ended, a gentleman named Allen from Madison, Wisconsin—he lives in Florida during the winter—came up to me and said, 'Wait a minute: I have something to give you.'"

What my dad said next might as well have been an atomic bomb exploding in my lap. "Curt, he got out his checkbook and handed me a check for $2,000! He said, 'I want to help your son. Give this to him.'"

Allen made it very clear that he didn't want anyone to know about this and that he wanted no credit for what he did. He may never realize the full impact he made on many individuals, especially one pastor and 12 student prayer warriors. I sent an e-mail to him explaining the best I could, but words can never express my joy at hearing what he did for me, all because he listened to the voice of the Holy Spirit. I'm sure that God has repaid him for his kindness many times over. Hopefully all Christians remember those inspired words "Truly, I say to you, as you did it to one of the least of these my brethren, you did it to me" (Matthew 25:40, RSV). In reality, Allen gave that money to God Himself, and what a privilege was his to give to our great Father in heaven, who gives so much to us. I now had no doubt whatsoever that God knew all, loved me, was in complete control, and knew exactly what I needed to rise above temptation.

Now, this would make a tremendous ending to this story, but God wasn't quite finished yet. Often we talk about the two sides of God's character, His love and His justice. His love side had been exhibited in a marvelous way, and it seemed that justice must come to the forefront as well. And so it did, for I had a call from Michael that following week. "Oh, Pastor, how are you?" he asked. "Do you have the money from the check so I can come and get it?"

"Hi, Michael," I responded. "I'm so glad to hear from you again. Why don't you come over to my home? Everything is taken care of."

I felt no more animosity toward him, but the desire for justice was in my heart. I suspect that most criminals rarely learn to forsake their evil ways unless the long arm of the law reaches their shoulder and brings them to justice. Michael sounded nervous, but he readily agreed to come by that Friday evening around sunset. He said he was so happy that he could now enroll in school, and I'd be lying if I told you I wasn't happy, too. I was also nervous and excited, and created a plan with Kim of what we would do and how things would transpire after he showed up. When Michael pulled up to the front door, Kim would go out the back door and get Andy Herold, our campus maintenance man. Andy was about six feet six, and I'm guessing around 260 pounds. He had a black belt in karate to boot. I figured he would do a fine job backing me up in this endeavor.

Michael was a smaller man, but I didn't know if his friend would show up with him, so I wanted to make sure our plan was fail-safe. After a few words of conversation we'd escort Michael and his partner in crime to my car and take them to the police station. We'd file charges, and justice would sooner or later be served. Unfortunately, if we had asked the police to come to our house to pick up a criminal, we might have waited a long, long time, as often no police cars are available. It is kind of strange to hear the police ask a citizen to come pick them up and take them to the criminals, but often that's the way things are in Kenya, with the lack of money to buy an adequate number of vehicles.

Friday evening finally came. I was nervous, but all my plans were in place and with God's help things would transpire appropriately. I stood by the window, looking out, hoping to see Michael walking down the street to our house. It began to get dark, and still he hadn't come. Vespers was at 7:30, and I hoped that he'd come before that so we could get to vespers on time. Finally about 7:15 I saw the lights of a car coming down the road. Looking carefully, I couldn't believe my eyes. Michael had rented a taxi! He was so confident that he was going to be rich by the end of that night that he actually rented an expensive taxi driver to bring him to my house for the money. As planned, Kim slipped out the back door as I opened the front. Michael had dressed quite nicely for the occasion and carried a nice briefcase. "Oh, Pastor, how are you this evening?" he asked. "I'm so glad to finally come and see you. God is so good."

I was ready too. "Michael, I am *soooo* happy to see you. God is wonderful, isn't He, to give us the desires of our hearts." I kept a straight face, knowing full well that we were on two completely different wavelengths, not to mention from two different planets of thought. "Come in, Michael, and sit down," I said calmly. "It's good to see you again."

He sat down, and I asked how he was doing. He was all smiles and asked about the money. About now, I remembered that God had brought me to this place to be a pastor and that I should never forget to do my duty. So I did what any good pastor would do in these circumstances. I gave Michael a full-blown sermon. I doubt you would ever guess what the sermon was about, so I'll let you in on it.

"Michael, you know that Jesus is coming again very soon, right?" I asked.

"Oh, yes, Pastor, very soon I believe," Michael responded. He seemed surprised that by now he wasn't already gone with the money.

"Michael, when Jesus comes He is going to look down at us here on this earth, and He will see everything that we have ever done in our lives. Jesus knows all, and He sees both the good and bad that we do. Jesus is our judge, Michael. You understand what a judge does?" I asked.

"Yes, Pastor, I understand what you are saying," Michael retorted, beginning to squirm just a bit in his chair.

"Michael," I continued, "Jesus will look in our hearts to see if we are following Him or the world. If we don't accept Him in our lives, then we will do bad things and go against God."

I'd just about reached the middle of my sermon when Andy came in, all six feet six and 260 pounds of him, and his eyes held a piercing gaze. He walked right in without knocking and stood directly next to where Michael was sitting. Respectful of the intense sermon I was giving Michael, he did not say a word. However, he did not take his eyes off the young man. I noticed that great drops of sweat had formed on Michael's brow and had begun to flow down his face. "Michael, do you know what I despise more than anything else?" I asked.

"No, Pastor. What do you despise more than anything else?" he asked nervously, eyeballing the Goliath who stood next to him looking like he was really, really hungry and was about to devour his supper.

It was at this point that the front door opened and in walked five of our night watchmen with their homemade bows and arrows and long dark-green overcoats. They too were quiet and respectful. Without a word they walked past the chair where Michael sat and surrounded it from behind. Then they just stood there, looking fierce.

I noticed that Michael was having difficulty swallowing and that streams of sweat now poured down his face. I hate to admit it, but while on the outside I was very serious, inside I felt vindicated. Michael was getting exactly what he deserved. I could hardly contain myself, but I felt it a must to finish my sermon. Just so I don't appear too unchristian in my approach to Michael, I did plan to visit him in prison, where I hoped he would forsake his ways and accept Jesus Christ. Unfortunately, I was not able to do so, but I do know that God has many, many ways of reaching His wayward children.

I did my best to drive home the final nail of truth into his heart. "Michael, you broke my trust. You lied to me and stole money from me. I know that you and your friend stole those checks from some unfortunate tourists."

"Oh, no, Pastor! I didn't steal from you. I would never do such a thing to you, Pastor!" Michael protested, knowing that the game was up.

"Michael, you are going to jail. You are going to have to pay for your theft and lying ways." When the inevitable seemed to sink in and the guards moved closer to take him to my car, Michael suddenly grabbed his briefcase, opened it in one swift motion, and reached inside. My first thought was that he had a gun and he was going to start shooting. Almost simultaneously, both Andy's and my hands shot toward the briefcase, closed it on Michael's hand, and pulled it away. I took it across the room while the guards grabbed hold of our thief. Opening the briefcase, I searched through everything. Fortunately, it held no gun or weapon of any kind. I breathed a sigh of relief as I set it down. Whether or not Michael was bluffing or he had brought a weapon with him and an angel had removed it we'll not know until we get to heaven, but either way God was looking out for us, and I was so thankful for His protection.

We put Michael into the back seat of the car between two night guards. Another guard sat on a small seat in the very back of the car. As we turned off campus, Michael pointed toward a man who was standing just outside the gate. He said it was his friend, who happened to be a bit smarter than he was. Later I found out that the man was the mastermind behind this scam. As we passed, he quickly turned and walked into the darkness. I figured it wasn't worth trying to go after him, for then we might lose Michael. Hopefully we could bring the police back, and they could find him. So we continued on to the police station, where I filed a report and they arrested Michael and began to rough him up.

In Kenya a person accused of a crime is considered guilty until proven innocent. Police often shoot first and ask questions later. I can't count the number of times I've seen news clips of police having shot and killed suspected thieves after a car chase that went on for some kilometers. By the time we'd completed the report and were walking to the car, I heard Michael yelling. It sounded as though he was being beaten. A pang of sorrow filled my heart, for even though I wanted justice, I never wanted him to be beaten.

It wasn't long after Michael's arrest that I heard from my friend at the exchange bureau. The $1,000 check had bounced too. But then God gave me one final nail of love in my coffin of lack of faith. My dad called and said that he was going to give me the other $1,000 to make up for my loss. What a God! What a loving, caring Father we have in heaven. And what a terrific dad! With amazement I think of David and wonder what event caused him to proclaim this truth about God recorded in Psalm 24:1: "The earth is the Lord's and the fulness thereof, the world and those who dwell therein" (RSV). God's love simply knows no bounds. It will not be stopped, for His riches are well beyond our comprehension, and He has thousands of ways to accomplish His will. When you love Him and surrender your will to His, that all-powerful love is yours.

Remember it well. God will not be stopped. His riches are your riches, just as His grace through Jesus is all yours.

After some months Michael was finally brought to trial. Going to court in Kenya is an unusual experience. When my case was called up before the judge, I walked up to stand on one side of the courtroom. At the same time Michael was brought in to stand on the other side. A couple of guards stood close by him. In Kenya the accused has the opportunity to question the accuser, which, of course, was me.

Michael looked over at me and started right in. "Isn't it true, Pastor, that you lied about all these accusations and it is you who has stolen? Isn't it true that you have stolen from me and you have lied about all this?"

My eyes opened wide with disbelief as I wondered how in the world he was going to impress the judge to believe that. When he finished with about four questions of that nature, I responded calmly and deliberately, "No." I don't think that either Michael, the judge, or anyone in the courtroom expected a one-word answer. Again, Michael accused me with slightly different words but the same intent. This time I said, "No. You are the one telling lies." After the third time of his using the same wording and tactics, the judge loudly told him to stop asking the same questions. She reminded him that he had only four more questions, and then he was finished. She also warned him that if he asked the same question one more time, he was through. I suspected that because he had nothing on me he would probably ask the same question yet again, and he did. At that the judge told him to shut up, and started ripping him verbally for not listening to her the first time.

Then the judge turned to me. With an unusual change of demeanor, she spoke words of wisdom that I will not soon forget. "Pastor DeWitt, God has given you a gift to help people. He brought you here to Kenya to give to our people. Please don't let this man take that gift away from you. God has blessed you, and you have blessed others. Don't stop because of what this man has done to you. Please don't stop giving to our people."

Then she looked from me to Michael. "This man is not even a Kenyan," she announced.

Turning to the guard, she directed, "Guard, lift up his shirt." The guard lifted Michael's shirt, and we saw that his vaccination mark was in a different spot from where Kenyans are vaccinated. Michael was actually Ugandan.

"Please, Pastor DeWitt, don't stop giving to our people," the judge pleaded. "We have so many poor Kenyans who need people like you to help them."

I was touched, to say the least. I never expected the judge to react in this way. I felt as though God was speaking through her to the depths of my soul, because He knew that I had made up my mind never to trust another Kenyan again. God has so many ways to speak to us, and this was one way that reached my heart.

At that point I knew that the judge would find Michael guilty. It took another year before his case came up again, but in the end a friend of mine who worked for the Central Intelligence Division and had helped in the arrest informed me that Michael had been sentenced to two years in prison and afterward would be deported to Uganda.

I never had the opportunity to witness to Michael and to bring him to Jesus. I can only pray that God somehow touched his heart and helped him see the error of his ways. Only God knows, but at least I can pray for Michael every day and God will continue to work on his heart. I know that God wants to save Michael as much as He wants to save me or anyone else on earth, and I hope to see him in heaven one day.

I learned many things from this experience. I learned that one has to use a lot of common sense and intelligence when helping others, especially when giving out money. I came to realize that everyone in this world isn't trustworthy, but that God still loves them. I know that good motives don't always protect a person from getting hurt, but that ultimately God is still in control and through it all *He* can still be trusted. Yes, over the next three years I found it very difficult to give money to people in need, but slowly God softened my heart until I gladly gave once again.

It was very difficult to have people knocking at my door week after week, asking for help to put their child through school. I recall the times mothers came with a sick child in their arms, having no money to pay for a doctor's visit. Sadly a dad who had AIDS came to us asking for money to take his children back to their village so that before he died he could make sure that they would be taken care of. Most of these needs are legitimate. The people are telling the truth, and still, how hard it is for those of us who have it to let go of that money. Many times I have given 200 or 300 shillings and patted myself on the back. One of these days our possessions, property, and homes are going to be worthless because we will be fleeing from infuriated mobs, and our lack of giving to the cause of God will rise up like a great mountain to crush us (see *Counsels on Stewardship,* p. 60). We will wish for another opportunity to give to God's cause, but it will be too late. The love of hanging on to our money may snuff out our lives, and we may be found wanting when it's all over. Now is the time to give as God has given to us. Not next week, not tomorrow, but now we should be parting with our money and possessions. God loves a cheerful giver, and He implores us not to be weary in well doing! (see 2 Corinthians 9:7; Galatians 6:9).

Until I went to Kenya, I never realized how selfish I really was. We Americans feel good when we put $1 or $5 in the offering plate, but we all make sure that we have three meals a day and we buy new clothes and shoes when ours begin to look a bit worn. We have our vehicles and homes but, like the Pharisees of old, we give out from our excess and not our hearts. Try not having anything to eat for two or three days—or sometimes a week! Try wearing the same ragged cloth partially covering your body, with no change of clothes in your closet. Closet? Many Kenyans have no home and sleep outside in alleys or near marketplaces with nothing. They have no water to drink, let alone for bathing.

Of course, many other countries face the same difficulties. It's a worldwide human problem, not just in Africa. Children and adults suffer all over the world.

Have you ever slept on the street? Try it. Experience getting beat up when someone gives you a piece of bread because other starving street urchins will take by force the crust you're trying to stuff into your hungry mouth. School? Forget it. It's more important to stay alive and eat than to sit in a classroom and learn. In Kenya one can see kids a mere 8 or 9 years old walking around the streets sniffing rubber cement glue because they're hooked and can't quit. Though they haven't eaten in three days, they'll buy glue before food, because they can't stop the addiction.

Do you know what the saddest part of all this is? We don't seem to care. We don't care because we've never seen it. We've never looked beyond our own hometown and fairly comfortable lives, and we have no clue how badly people suffer, or else we're too busy padding our own lives to think about anyone else. May God help us be merciful to others and actively love all of God's children, even as God shows us mercy and love in spite of ourselves.

Chapter 5

A Spitting Cobra Visits Church

The nasty dragon, that old cobra-like snake called Satan,
attempts to deceive all of us who live in this world. His temptations may
look enticing at first, but in the end his venom will paralyze us, and
we will pay a stiff price (Revelation 12:9, PCRV; Proverbs 14:12, PCRV).

I f I had to put my finger on one particular thing that makes Kenya special to me, it would be difficult not to focus on its many different creatures. And while I love all the wild animals native to Kenya, none give me an adrenaline rush like the snakes. This country could be considered a herpetologist's heaven!

As a boy I always enjoyed snakes and have many fond memories of garter snakes and blue racers. I recall that my parents had a book about Africa that had amazing pictures of the different creatures native to the continent. Many Friday evenings found me sitting quietly on the floor of the study, looking at every single picture in this book. I was fascinated by the lions and cheetahs, but one certain picture was my favorite. It was the picture of a cobra. That picture literally made my blood run cold, for I'd stare at the page almost to the point of being afraid even to touch the ink on the paper lest it come to life and I get bitten by this poisonous snake.

I often wondered if I would ever get the chance to see one up close, but always concluded that it wasn't likely, as I could never afford a visit to Africa. So I settled for the picture in the safari book instead.

Now, I know that most people think snakes are downright nasty and that the only good snake is a dead one. But snakes—just as many other dangerous creatures, such as sharks and crocodiles—are quite misunderstood. Yes, I know that God put a curse on snakes after Satan used one to plunge our world into misery, but I don't recall reading in Genesis that God said that *all* snakes should be killed. I believe that just like all other creatures on earth, snakes were created by God, and surely He must love them as much as He does the rest of His creation. Just think for a moment what would happen if all snakes were killed. I'm not a scientist, but I figure that we'd all die from disease, because rats and mice would soon overrun the world! We need snakes, and in my estimation they do much more good than bad.

Despite my interest in and my feelings about snakes, one thing is certain—Kenyans hate snakes. When a Kenyan sees a snake slithering across a rocky terrain, any man who is brave enough comes no closer than 20 feet, grabs rocks and stones, and begins the onslaught. Now, granted, they miss quite often, but they'll keep it up until a lucky throw slams into the snake's head. But the stones keep flying until the snake has stopped all movement. Only then the bravest of the brave gets close enough to poke it with a long stick. If the snake doesn't move, he hits it over the head about 10 times to make sure it's quite dead. You've heard the saying "I wouldn't touch that with a 10-foot pole!" Well, that saying is surely true in Kenya when it comes to snakes. Most poles I've seen in men's hands are about 11 feet long. Let me tell you, if a man has succeeded in killing a snake and has it dangling toward the end of his stick, he is almost revered by others. It's almost as though he holds the same distinction as Samson back in biblical times.

Some of my Kenyan friends told me that many people feel that a person who catches snakes has some kind of magical power or witchcraft, and they're respected for that. I caught many snakes during my six years in Kenya, and I was told that some local thieves were afraid to break into my house. They feared that I might have a dangerous snake in the house that would bite them *or* that perhaps I might put a curse on them. And even though *I* knew that God was my protector, I never rushed out to set them straight.

As I said, there are many different kinds of snakes in Africa, and

I'm going to tell you about some of them. First, there are Cape wolf snakes. These snakes are perfectly harmless and very comfortable being held by people. They have long canine-like teeth that they use to hold their prey. Unfortunately, there is a species of snakes that looks a lot like wolf snakes but has serious venom that can kill. These are known as burrowing asps. One of the asp species, a small-scaled burrowing asp, is known in Somalia as the Father of 10 Minutes or the Snake of Seven Steps. These curious nicknames indicate that if you're bitten you either have 10 minutes to live or you can run seven steps to get help before you collapse and die. According to the book *A Field Guide to the Reptiles of East Africa* antivenom is ineffective against the bite of the burrowing asps.

The unusual thing about asps is that they have very strong neck muscles. Even though you might hold them carefully behind the head—as you would other snakes—they can jerk-twist their head sideways, move their fangs to the side, and prick your hand. Hence, they've been given two more names: Side-stabbing Snakes and Stiletto Snakes. Most of those bitten by this small snake are handlers unaware of their ability to twist and bite. I'll never forget the first time I carefully caught what I deemed a harmless snake—but discovered it might not be so tame. After comparing its appearance to species pictured in the snake book, I really began to sweat. You see, the snake's shape and markings led me to the asp species for the first time. Fortunately, as I studied it further I realized that it was a Cape wolf snake, but let me tell you, I thanked God for His protection in spite of my ignorance. During my time in Kenya I never saw an asp, and it's probably fortunate for me.

Another snake that gets a lot of attention and has quite a reputation worldwide is the black mamba, scientifically labeled as *Dendroaspis polylepis*. It is known as the most poisonous snake in Africa and listed as one of the top 12 most poisonous in all the world. I have seen this snake only two or three times, usually from a distance. These snakes are quite formidable, as they can grow up to 10 to 12 feet (three to four meters) long. They're known as the fastest snake in the world—traveling in excess of 11 or 12 miles (18 to 20 kilometers) per hour. Can you imagine seeing a mamba speed along the ground with his head raised more than four feet (one meter)? That would strike fear in the bravest of hearts! There are rumors that the black mamba actually attacks human beings, but very few of the stories have been verified.

The black mamba is not black at all, and is wrongly named. It's the inside of their mouths that are actually black. The snake is usually light gray, olive, or brownish gray, and the skin can get much lighter near the coastal areas of Kenya. I have not caught one of these, and I'm not sure if I'd have the nerve to catch an adult. When someone approaches in a vehicle, they usually move away very quickly, and it's probably a good thing. Black mambas are large, nervous, and willing to bite. There is antivenom to be had if you're close enough to a hospital. Without serum, the bite of the black mamba is nearly 100 percent fatal. Rumors have it that a person dies within five to 30 minutes after being bitten, but that is hardly the case. According to the *Field Guide to the Reptiles of East Africa* death is unusual if the victim gets to a hospital within a couple of hours after being bitten. For sure you don't want to delay getting to a hospital, especially if the victim is a small child. They could die within a much shorter period of time.

The most dangerous snake in Kenya, and I believe in all Africa, is the puff adder, appropriately labeled *Bitis arietans*. These snakes are quite impressive and have an attitude that John McEnroe would be proud to possess. They grow to be only three to four feet (one meter) long, but they can be 20 inches (50 centimeters) or larger in circumference. They have nasty hinged fangs and aren't afraid to use them. Puff adders are some of the most dangerous snakes in Africa because they like to rest in dark places, such as under beds or in dark corners, where an unsuspecting African can accidentally step on them—prompting a quick and deadly defense. They also sit quietly when approached, giving no warning of their presence.

A very good Masai friend of mine lost a stepmother because that very thing happened in her home. Typically you have plenty of time to get to a hospital, and seldom die before six hours or more pass.

But if you happen to live out in the savannah with no vehicle to quickly take you for help, then your life is in greater danger.

I saw a number of puff adders in Kenya and even attempted to catch two of them, but I was a bit nervous about it. I did succeed in grabbing the lower half, but quickly let go because they are so short and stout and have a lightning strike. It didn't help that my wife was yelling at me to *stop*. Unfortunately, I didn't have my snake tongs with me either time.

Puff adders are quite beautiful in color and pattern, especially the yellow phase that I saw in the Nairobi Game Park. Even though this snake has large venom sacs, not all people die from a puff adder bite, but it is a significant percentage, so all should be wary when Mr. *Bitis* is around.

The most unusual and most fascinating snake that I've ever found is the Northeast African carpet viper. This tiny snake grows to about 10 inches or so in length, but what it lacks in size it more than makes up for in spirit and potency of venom. We found a few of these in the Lake Baringo area, where they hide under rocks during the day. When this snake gets angry, it forms a series of C-shaped coils. The coils shift against each other in opposite directions, producing a sound much like water falling on a very hot pan. At the same time, the snake may be moving backward or forward, and if further agitated will strike continuously and vigorously (*Field Guide to the Reptiles of East Africa,* p. 484). I agitated one a couple of times, and was amazed at how it rushed toward me—all eight inches of it—and struck over and over. Thus once again, I was reminded of David and Goliath. This brave snake's display didn't work, and I carefully captured it anyway; but it was nonetheless most impressive.

There was one particular snake that I wanted to see more than any other, and if you read the beginning of this book you've probably figured out which it was. When we moved to Kenya, high on my priority to-do list was to see and hopefully hold a *Naja nigricollis,* a black-necked spitting cobra. I didn't have to wait very long for my childhood dream to come true.

During the first half of our first year in Kenya the opportunity came. Walking to the administration building one morning, I noticed two students running around behind the church. I quickly saw that they were of the opposite sex, so I thought I had better go and check it out, because you never know what a young man and woman might be planning even if they're right next to the church.

As I rounded the side of the building, I saw them near the side door. And no, they weren't kissing or even holding hands. In fact, I think they were completely oblivious to each other's presence. "Hey, guys," I said. "What's up?"

None too calmly Nick Delgado quickly retorted, "A snake! A snake, Pastor Curt! It just went under the door into the church."

"Could you tell what kind it was?" I asked, feeling a little excited myself. Remember, I'd wanted to see a snake in Africa ever since I was about 5 years old.

"I'm pretty sure it was a spitting cobra!"

At that my heart started pounding and I felt my brain pulse with excitement. The adrenaline was pumping beyond anything I'd ever felt before. I was ecstatic. Up until then I'd only heard about one or two incidents with black-necked spitting cobras. The main thing I grasped was that they can spit their venom, and they have tremendous aim even up to 10 to 12 feet (three to four meters) away. If their aim is correct, the animal or human is temporarily blinded, and I've been told the venom stings and causes severe pain and swelling. So it was with my heart in my throat that I went back to the front of the church and quietly opened the door. I had no idea where the snake could be, but I was not about to pass up this opportunity. Two students, Lloyd Mabuto and Nick, slipped through the foyer behind me. Slowly we crept down the center aisle. I looked back and forth, under every one of the pews, making sure this snake didn't surprise us. I figured that it wouldn't go over too well with parents if their kids were bitten, so as I carefully made my way to the front of the church I kept the students back behind me. Several times I realized that I was holding my breath, so I let it out slowly and quietly. There was no doubt that you could have heard a pin drop in the church sanctuary or even a small drop of sweat drip off of a forehead.

By this time other students had gathered outside the side door where the snake had gone in, just in case it tried to escape the same way. Closer and closer we came to the rostrum, looking around everywhere, figuring that by the time we actually saw the snake it would have grown to maybe 25 feet (seven to eight meters) long with gigantic fangs that could bite through anything. I also figured that by then it could spit its nasty venom at least 40 feet.

And then Nick spoke. Loudly. "There it is by the microphone cords."

I quickly looked that direction. Sure enough, there it was. At first glance it looked quite large—four or five feet (one and a half meters) long. I told the students to stay back, but I wanted to get a closer look at this incredible piece of creation. I couldn't believe that my dream was becoming a reality! No matter how scared I was, I was not going to let this snake get away. I was determined to catch it at any cost.

By this time my heart was hammering away at least 120 beats per minute. I inched to within about 12 feet (four meters) of the cobra, then stopped, for it had suddenly become agitated. It lifted its head, spread its hood, and glared directly at me. In that split second I simply froze, enthralled with its beauty. Suddenly something *zoomed* toward me, directly at my eyes, like a small bullet shot out of a gun. Before I could blink or turn my head, something struck my temple, missing my left eye by less than one-fourth inch (one-half centimeter). The snake had done what all black-necked spitting cobras are good at doing. It aimed its hinged fangs directly at my eyes and spit!

I know that it just wanted to discourage me from coming any closer, *and it worked*. I was wearing glasses, so I felt that my eyes were somewhat protected, but let me tell you—the accuracy of its aim overwhelmed me, and I leaped back almost into the arms of the two boys. Quickly wiping away the venom, I yelled for Lloyd to grab a broom or mop or anything that I could use to protect my eyes from this worthy foe.

Lloyd ran back to the janitor's closet, grabbed a mop, and raced back to the front as I kept a wary eye on this snake. I grabbed the mop and shoved the mop head between the cobra's head and my eyes, doing my best to watch the rest of its body. Slipping closer, I realized that the snake was spitting one blob of venom after another. I could feel it hitting the mop, but even so, I crept to within four feet of it. At this point the cobra must have figured that I wasn't going to back down, for it quickly dropped and slithered toward the three-inch gap at the bottom of the door. Its head and upper body made it out before I pinned the rest of its body to the church floor with the head of the mop. I could feel it writhing to get free, so I pressed as hard as I could to keep it there.

On the other side of the door the guys were yelling that the snake was outside. When I realized that it couldn't escape, I said to Lloyd, "Quick, hold this mop down and don't let it get away! I'll run around and get it by the head." I might just as well have said, "Lloyd, quick! Come and hold on to this 525-pound [200-kilogram] lion's tail until I get a rope!"

"Oh, Pastor Curt, Pastor Curt! No, I can't hold him! What if he gets away and bites me?" Lloyd cried. *"Pastor Curt, ohhh, ohhhhh!"* He was in a full-blown panic attack, the mop still in his hands.

I raced around to where a crowd of guys had clustered near the door. Much to my dismay, I saw that one of the boys had pinned down the cobra's head with a stick. The head looked quite flat and I was sure they had killed it. I didn't see how any snake could withstand such pressure. Carefully taking the stick from the student's hands, I let up a bit on the pressure. To my relief, the snake moved slightly. I was so mentally challenged that my hands were shaking badly, but I carefully reached down and grabbed the snake behind its head. At the same time I yelled for Lloyd to let go of the mop. Let me tell you, before the handle hit the church floor he was out the front door.

There I stood, holding my first cobra! I felt a smile split my face as I showed it off to the students. They were all quite relieved and happy. The snake measured just under four feet (one meter) long. It was a nice specimen, and I took it around the campus to show it to everyone who cared to see. The reaction of most of the Kenyan workers surprised me. Some of them were angry that I hadn't killed the snake, and all of them stayed a far distance away from it. They would hardly even look at this hideous death machine, let alone touch it!

I finally decided it was time to get in the car and drive down the road to the bottom of the big hill, where there was a river and lots of trees. There I'd let the snake go free. So a few moments later found me holding the snake with my left hand while driving down the road with my right. I suppose that wasn't very smart, but I was too excited to think clearly. Finding and capturing the cobra had been a wonderful experience.

After that day I caught many cobras who found their way to the Maxwell Academy campus. I don't know exactly how many I caught and released in the game park, but it was probably pushing 15 or 20. The largest one was approximately five feet six inches (one and a half meters) long. The smallest was only about eight inches (20 centimeters). My wife and I had a lot of fun with that tiny guy one Sabbath afternoon. Sometimes catching the larger ones meant a lengthy battle. But I always wore goggles and used either a stick or snake tongs, which were a tremendous help. Because of their spitting, spitting cobras are by far the most difficult snake to capture. I received many venom stains on a few shirts, but fortunately they came out in the wash.

Once as my wife and I were trying to transport a problematic cobra, I was holding it behind the head and attempting to place it in a garbage bin. Kim's job was holding the bin as I crept toward her, the head of the snake pointing directly at her face. Even though I had my thumb pressing on the snake's head, it spit right into her mouth! As you can imagine, she about had a fit. Call me heartless, call me crazy, but I burst out laughing. It was a comical sight—Kim spitting all the way to the house and washing out her mouth over and over. But she's a good sport, and later on we had a good laugh about it. She said that the venom was very bitter. The venom doesn't hurt the skin. It works only if it goes into the eyes or the bloodstream. Other than the bitterness, she had no ill effects, thank the good Lord.

And by the way, I *did* get the snake into the bin.

You know, these cobras are much like Satan. It's rather uncanny how snakes, especially the black-necked spitting cobra, so closely resemble Satan in character and ability. These snakes are *always* dangerous no matter where they are located, just as Satan is *always* on the prowl, searching for victims. Just like the snake, Satan can never be trusted—not under any circumstances. Both the cobra and Satan are quite deceptive, whether lying in the sun or waiting around the next corner with a tempting thought or suggestion.

Beware of that old serpent called Satan! Snakes warrant respect because of their fangs and venom. We must be wary of the devil's ability to poison our minds with his venom that attacks the spiritual system of the body. We must lose confidence in our thinking that we can handle the danger, and most assuredly must respect Satan's ability to destroy us when we stand alone.

After catching that first cobra, I told myself that the day I stop fearing these poisonous snakes I would quit catching them, for surely I would end up being bitten. At all times we must step back and let the great snake controller, Jesus Christ, take charge. Only He knows how to handle this evil one. How many times have I been enticed by some sinful temptation? How many times have you stepped too close to evil, thinking that it was something interesting when at that very moment your eyes were blinded by his deceptive venom?

Satan used a snake at the tree of knowledge of good and evil to bring Eve and our world under his domain. Let us all beware of Satan and flee to the tree of life, where stands Jesus, our protector and Savior. God's truth will keep us free from Satan's poisoning of our minds. It is the truth from God's Word that will protect us. We would all do better if we would go to Jesus and stay with Him 24/7. Let us study the truth from God's Word, lest God allow us to believe lies with all our heart because we have refused to love and embrace the truth (see 2 Thessalonians 2:10, 11, TLB).

Chapter 6

Camping Out in the Masai Mara

You should always take the difficult path because the opposite trail is easy and not challenging at all. Everyone else goes that way, but sooner or later all will come to a dead end, and there will be no turning back for any of them. If you look forward to living forever with your Savior, then walk the narrow and difficult path. He will lead you to eternal life, and don't worry about trials along the way. He has already planned ahead (Matthew 7:13, 14, PCRV).

After I was married, often while my wife and I were hanging out with her family I'd listen to their memories of camping in the Masai Mara. I'd sit there with an incredulous look on my face as I thought to myself, *Man, these people's elevators definitely don't go all the way to the top floor!*

How in the world could someone camp out in the middle of a game reserve with massive lions and attitudinal leopards, not to mention larger-than-life elephants roaming all around them? Kim would see me shaking my head in the nonaffirmative direction and ask, "Curt, wouldn't you like to camp out like that?"

"Yeah sure," I'd retort. "Just as long as I have two .357 magnums in my holster with plenty of ammunition. I'd *love* to camp out in the Mara!" Then they'd all laugh and relate stories about going to the "bathroom" in the middle of the night under an acacia tree that happened to contain a snoozing leopard, and other hair-raising tales. After listening to them for an hour I figured either they were *really* lucky that they were still alive or that God felt sorry for them and their lack of common sense and protected them because of it.

Who would ever dream that one day I too would lose my common sense and be just like my wife and her family? Believe it or not, it happened! I will never forget the first time we camped out in the Mara. Of course, it was all very exciting while it was still daylight (although I paid careful attention to the bushes around our tent). And I carried a hatchet and a big hunting knife with me at all times, unless we were riding around in the vehicle hoping to see wild animals. But when that sun slipped down over the horizon, things changed dramatically. I was reminded of one *very* important fact when it comes to animals, especially nocturnal ones with big teeth. They can see after dark, and I can't!

I can tell you one thing about that first camping trip. I slept maybe 20 minutes total the whole weekend. When you are by yourselves in the vast savannah beneath a breathtaking star-filled sky, it is truly an incredible, if sometimes eerie, feeling. There is nothing quite like it. It's just you, the animals, the sky, and God all together in His world.

The Mara is amazing for many reasons, but one reason in particular keeps bringing people back. Just when you think you've seen everything you could possibly see . . . just when you say, "Man, we'll never see anything better than this!" . . . the next time you visit you hear yourself repeating those same words: "Man, we'll never see anything better than *this*!"

The Mara gives you a taste of heaven on earth, because it's exactly what I picture when I think of being in heaven. Every day we'll be saying, "Wow! Life can't get any better than this!" But with each passing day—with each passing moment—new and still more glorious things will please the eyes and hearts of God's children.

People go to the Masai Mara for one reason in particular, and that is to see the incredible animals. Dozens of different kinds of animals live in the Mara, but some seem more special than others. For starters, most tourists hope that they can spot the big five: lion, leopard, elephant, rhinoceros, and Cape buffalo. Any of these five are quite impressive, especially when you're parked about 20 feet (six meters) away. But who can ignore others, such as the cheetah, hippopotamus, giraffe, crocodile, wildebeest, zebra, and many other herbivores?

Somehow more than any of the other animals, there is something most intriguing about the cats. Tourists would be very unhappy if they went on a safari and never got a snapshot of a lion. They would go home completely unsatisfied. But if a tourist saw a lion and leopard but didn't see any other animals, they'd still feel happy with the outcome of their trip. The leopard, in particular, is quite special. Its ability to blend in with its background makes it the most elusive of the cats. Many times we'd look into a tree with the naked eye and see nothing. But when we checked out the tree with binoculars, there sat a leopard that had been staring at us the whole time. It quickly became our favorite animal to search for.

One late afternoon we were watching a leopard that seemed quite used to vehicles and people. It lay in a typical gourd tree, one with wide, spread-out branches and lots of shade. The leopard was probably about 12 feet (four meters) above the ground, contentedly relaxing. We were parked directly beneath it. With our roof hatch open, we stood quietly taking pictures and just enjoying ourselves immensely. The leopard occasionally flicked lazy eyes toward us as we tried to figure out if it was a male or female. Time passed. As it neared sundown I decided to make a racket so the leopard would stand up. But after making all the ferocious lion noises I could muster, the leopard—not convinced in the least—still lay sprawled over that branch. I looked around the car for something to toss toward the cat, and saw my son's wrist rocket, which is a fancy slingshot. My eyes lit up as I grabbed it and a piece of hard candy lying on the dashboard. I figured that I'd gently shoot that piece of candy at the backside of the cat. That'd rouse it to stand up, and then we could tell if it was a male or female.

So forgetting how powerful a wrist rocket actually is, I pulled back, aimed for that spotted rump, and let it fly. My plan worked. Boy, did it work! The leopard leaped to its feet, glared directly at me, curled its lip above large fangs, and snarled horribly!

I'm dead, I thought. *I'm already dead. That cat's going to kill me.*

I saw it lurch my direction, its muscles coiled and ready to spring. I knew there was no way I could get the hatch closed in time if it decided to jump. I watched, frozen, as it did jump—to the ground, loping off in another direction.

I let out my breath, relieved that I could actually breathe again, and wiped the sweat off my brow. At that point in my life I figured that maybe it's best to leave wild animals alone and just take pictures. And by the way, it *was* a female, which I'd figured all along.

On a different weekend, we found ourselves in the same vicinity hoping to see the same leopard, for they are quite territorial animals. We weren't disappointed. There she was walking through the grass, completely unaware that nearby was the guy who had shot her in the gluteus maximus many months before. I felt very thankful that leopards don't have the memories of elephants. Then as we watched her walk around the area, we saw a safari van carrying some European tourists pull up across the wayside from us. We figured that they'd stopped because they saw that we'd been sitting in one place for quite a while. In any game park, whenever you see a vehicle parked at one location for more than three minutes, you assume that they're watching a pride of lions, a leopard, or maybe a couple of cheetahs. Of course, sometimes we've raced over to a stopped vehicle only to discover that they had a flat tire or were stuck in the mud.

As we watched this elegant leopard slip through the tall grass between us and the van we saw the van door slide open, and two men and two women got out. OK, that wasn't too smart. In fact, it was downright dangerous. We immediately tried to call out that a leopard was between them and us, but we'd hardly opened our mouths when the men strode to the front of the van—facing the opposite direction from us—and proceeded to water the grass. What happened next nearly caused us to fall out of our vehicle. The two women, oblivious to the fact that there were people directly behind them (not to mention one big leopard), pulled down their pants and squatted down at the back of the van—nearly blinding us with two ultrawhite full moons!

Amazingly, they continued talking and laughing with each other as if they were fully clothed and leaning across a table having tea. We, on the other hand, were in a bit of shock and amazement as we tried to shield our eyes. We decided it was best to graciously wait with our warning until they'd finished their important business. Of course, by then we'd completely lost sight of the leopard, who after witnessing the tourists' immodesty most likely decided she'd seen quite enough for one day and went to find some shade and a pair of sunglasses.

Each time we camped out in the Mara, we always prayed that we would have visitors during the night. We would park our vehicle within 20 feet (six meters) or less of our tent's entrance, and if we heard noises that resembled animal sounds, we'd carefully sneak out to the car and turn on its spotlights so we could get a clear view. One night we were awakened to a whole herd of Cape buffalo eating all around the tent. Let me tell you, their snorting sounds an awful lot like lions on the prowl, and the rest of that night I'd find my eyes wide open, a hatchet in my hands, listening to see if these animals had the capability to open zippered tents!

Another time, when we were camping on the Sand River, the sun had just set beautifully behind the hills when I was startled to see a hyena standing beside our tent calmly eating. Now, hyenas are just as fearsome as any cat, but for some reason I didn't feel afraid, even though I stood just eight feet from him. Apparently unafraid as well, he glanced at me a few times. When he finished his meager meal, he quietly strolled off over a knoll. That was a special moment and what camping in the Mara is all about—grasping a moment with one of God's wild creatures without losing your life.

Our most awesome animal encounter came while we camped at the research station campsite. The first night on this trip we heard a grunting noise coming toward our camp from along a creekbed. We listened as the sound was repeated every minute or two, each time seeming closer and closer. Both Kim and I thought that it was a couple of lions, because it sounded to us as if there were two of them, one on the other side of the creek answering the other. We figured it was mating season. For some reason, probably because it was late, we didn't go and check things out. The next night we again heard the same grunting sound, but this time it sounded like only one animal. Kim and I were ready. Slipping out of the tent, we quietly got in the car and opened the top hatch, then waited with our million-candle-watt spotter in hand. Our adrenaline pumped into high gear as the grunting came closer and even closer. When we heard a deep grunt that sounded as if it was nearly across from us, I pointed the spotter directly at the sound and flicked on the switch. To our amazement, there stood a magnificent male leopard who acted as if he owned the whole park! Payday!

The leopard was not more than 30 feet (nine meters) away, basking in the rays of the bright light. He stretched his legs once or twice, looking very much like he was our house cat wanting to rub on a leg and say hello. After a couple of minutes the magnificent animal quietly padded off toward the creek as we counted our blessings, thanking the good Lord for what had just happened.

One of our funniest camping moments came when my brother, Craig, happened to be visiting. It was noon, and we were at the same campsite we'd seen the leopard sometime before, when suddenly our campout took an interesting turn.

We were all sitting around the fire pit, eating our lunch and having a good time talking about the animals we'd seen. I was facing Craig, my back to the creek below. I distinctly remember that he had just put a spoonful of food in his mouth and was looking my direction when he shot to his feet, every hair on his head standing straight up.

Now, because Craig's mouth was filled with food, I wasn't exactly sure what words were trying to force their way out or even what he was pointing at, but it contained a strong element of shock, fear, and surprise. I recall a couple of the strangled, blurted words, such as *"whaaaat?"* and *"dude,"* and *"how close are we supposed to get?"* Was it a local Masai man with leprosy walking out of the woods toward our camp?

I turned around, expecting to see a whole pride of man-eating lions, but, much to my delight, I saw four elephants on our side of the creek. They were walking out from among the trees and coming our direction. I can't say that I blame my brother for his reaction. After all, elephants are large and strong and have been known to kill puny humans who have ventured too close. It's not like elephants coming to lunch is an everyday occurrence. But judging by the relaxed state of our visitors, I knew we weren't in any immediate danger, unless, of course, Craig kept making those loud sputtering sounds. I quickly explained the importance of not making loud and irritating noises when elephants are nearby, and Craig quieted down at once. We silently watched a mother elephant with three younger ones amble by as though they had not a care in the world. They were only about 50 feet (15 meters) away from where we stood. What another taste of heaven!

When you live only three or four hours from the Masai Mara and that is your wife's favorite place in the entire world, it becomes very easy for a husband to plan a special getaway weekend to celebrate special occasions. Plus, it saves a lot of money. During one of those October birthdays I decided that we would plan a nice camping trip to Kim's favorite home away from home. So we packed everything up on a Friday afternoon, fully expecting it to be a wonderful weekend. We were about 20 miles (30 kilometers) from the main gate of the game reserve, happily going along in our trusty Mitsubishi Pajero, when we suddenly heard a funny noise near the front tire, and the car began bump-bump-bumping along. I stopped as quickly as I could and got out, expecting to see a flat tire. But much to my surprise, a tie rod seemed to be broken, as the tire stared blankly at me from an unusual angle. This had never happened before, and I knew that I had no idea how to fix it even if I had the right tools, so there we sat waiting for a passing vehicle. Sure enough, in about 10 minutes a tourist van drove up, and Kim got in to get some help at one of the lodges.

"What a start to a birthday weekend," I said to our kids, who sat staring glumly out the window as the van drove off in a cloud of dust. I wasn't very happy, but not nearly as unhappy as my wife! So we sat waiting for Mom and Masai AAA to come back and fix our car—hopefully before nightfall. But the day wore on, and the sun started sinking toward the western horizon. Still there was no sight of any rescue vehicle with my wife inside frantically waving to us. We decided to sing some songs, but after about two we figured that our throats were too dry to continue. It didn't help that as darkness settled over us we were in an area that contained lions and other wild, hungry creatures. Finally about four hours later we saw some headlights coming our way, which proved to be Kim and company. As the guys looked at our disabled vehicle, I asked her why it took so long to come back. So she related everything. I could only stand incredulously transfixed, not believing that a birthday weekend could end up so eventful.

About two and a half miles (four kilometers) down the road the battery had fallen out of the tourist van engine, and the van had come to an abrupt stop. Everyone got out to wait for the battery to be put back in, and while the driver was putting it in its regular place, the van started rolling down the hill. You see, it lacked a working handbrake. After chasing the van and making sure that that wouldn't happen again, the driver put the battery back, and they made it to the lodge. There Kim made arrangements to come back and pick us up and hopefully to get the car fixed. Two men and my wife then jumped into a 4 by 4 and headed back to where we sat dismally singing the blues. Believe it or not, within two miles (three kilometers) down the road the gas tank fell off the car! Of course, by this time it was completely dark, and when I say "dark," I mean really dark! Remember that out in the middle of nowhere, far away from any light pollution, it gets *very* dark. They needed to figure out how to tie up the gas tank, but neither one had a flashlight. So they had to radio for another 4 by 4 to come help. Somehow they were able to get the tank to stay up, and they started driving back about five miles (eight kilometers) per hour—about the same speed as a fast walk. They then met the other vehicle, and Kim switched places, and—at last—here she was. After driving to a nearby Masai village in search of someone to watch our car throughout the night, we finally made it back to the lodge.

I knew that one day down the road we would all laugh at this fiasco, as it really was simply amazing that so many things could go wrong. We decided that it would be quite difficult for us to set up camp in the dark, so we reluctantly stayed at the Sarova Lodge for the night. It wasn't far from the campsite, and we'd set up camp the next morning. Praise the Lord, I hadn't forgotten our credit card.

The next morning we all felt upbeat and decided that the whole weekend wasn't ruined yet, and we were going to make the best of the rest of it. After a mechanic fixed our car, we finally pulled into our favorite camping spot and unloaded everything. It was a beautiful morning, and I knew that God was still going to pour out His blessings in spite of what had already occurred. I got out the tent bag, laid the tent out as I always did, then went to get the tent poles. I looked in the bag but didn't see the poles anywhere. *Surely this can't be happening, can it?* I grimly thought. I looked around at my wife, bless her heart, and tried to figure out how to say what I had to say in a more positive sort of way. I came up empty, and she looked over at me wondering why I was standing in one place and not putting up the tent.

I ho-hummed around and finally said quietly, "I forgot the tent poles."

By this time we decided it was a good idea just to head home and maybe start all over, but we ended up spending that night at another lodge and actually survived this almost-unbelievable weekend. It's safe to say that neither of us will ever forget that birthday weekend and how costly it became!

It's days like these that we need God. Maybe you've heard this expression, one vital to our survival: *Before you face the day, face God.*

I don't recall who first said it, but I know that on some days everything that can go wrong does. Satan is at work in this world, and you and I must be prepared for anything to happen, because it usually does, especially if you are living in Kenya! The truth of the matter is this: If God is with you, it doesn't matter if the whole world collapses. Everything will end up OK because our Father is still in control. Don't ever forget it. Trials are a must for each one of us. Without trials, we would cease to realize our need of Christ.

The next time you're having a terrible day, look to Jesus and thank Him for the reminder that you need Him in your life. Then feel His arms of love hold you close. Even though your day has fallen apart you will know that you rest safely in the arms of the God of the universe.

One of the most fascinating things to see while camping in the Mara is the crossing of the wildebeest and zebra. People come from all over the world to see the migration of these animals that start in the Serengeti and go through the Masai Mara. Driven only by instinct, thousands and thousands cross over the Mara River. You never know exactly when any particular group will cross, and so a lot of patience is required. It took us more than four years to finally witness The Crossing to a small degree.

One midmorning we were driving on some side roads along the river when up ahead we noticed some vehicles parked some distance from the river. We'd been looking for the usual lions, leopards, and cheetahs, and so we went over their direction. But before we reached them we came upon a couple of lions sitting in tall grass not far from the river's edge. We'd heard many times that lions would wait on the other side of an area where animals cross, and pick off easy meals. As we drove slowly past the lions we came to a vehicle that sat facing the river. And on the other side of the river we saw a mass of wildebeest moving about nervously, as if they were ready to be on the move. The driver of the tourist van almost angrily waved us to stay back as we attempted to go around him. It was at that point that we realized that all these vehicles waiting near the river knew that the animals were about to cross. So we stopped where we were and waited with the rest of them.

We saw some of the leading wildebeests walk to the edge of a cliff that rose about 20 feet (six meters) above the river. And so we waited. In about five minutes The Crossing began, with the large animals jumping over the cliff's edge into the water. Suddenly we heard engines roar to life as the other vehicles raced toward the river's edge where the animals would attempt to run up the opposite side from where they entered. We pulled up and videotaped the whole process. At first it was quite exciting. We'd waited a long four years to see this wonderful sight, but it wasn't too long before we grew sick at heart. We assumed that we'd see crocodiles in the area, but we didn't. They weren't at this particular crossing. What we did see was the bank on the near side of the river get wet and muddy from the thousands of hooves climbing out on it. The wildebeest lucky enough to be near the front of the herd had no problems. But those unfortunate animals near the midway point or farther back didn't fare quite so well. We watched with growing horror as the first of the unlucky wildebeests struggled to gain footing in this slippery, muddy area. Many times it almost made it, only to fall back into the water as its strength slowly ebbed away. The water's strong current took over from there, tenaciously pulling the creature downriver and beneath the water's surface. It was very sad to see the wildebeest's head sink lower and lower. Finally, only its mouth broke the water's surface as it furiously fought to hang on to life, only to succumb to the horrific dark side of nature's ways.

After witnessing many more carcasses floating downstream, we decided that we'd seen enough and quietly pulled away to go back to our campsite.

After seeing our first crossing, I understand better how God must feel as He looks down on our small, shadowed world. His people gather together by the millions, ready to jump into the dark cold water called The Point of No Return. How God's heart breaks as He watches, desperately hoping that His children will turn around and take the narrow path that leads to life. He has worked night and day impressing us to trust Him and to study His Word so that we will not follow the countless others who are oblivious to the terrible result of their choices. It's the blind leading the blind, and yes, both shall die beneath the waves.

Those leading wildebeests remind me of the leaders in this world. Millions of people look to their leaders without so much as a glance in God's Word to see if, in fact, they are being led to Jesus or led astray. If a trusted leader says, "Follow me" or "Go ahead and jump!" or "Trust me, it's safe," the masses follow without any hesitation. Only too late they realize the inevitable truth. Now I understand why the undershepherds will howl in that day (see Jeremiah 25:34-38). I see why Jesus takes leadership so seriously among us. Now I better comprehend why it's important for me to direct my eyes to Jesus and the Word instead of on myself. I may be a pastor, but I am fallible and make mistakes. Jesus is the only one who will lead every soul safely to His kingdom.

Young or old, whoever you are, keep your eyes on Jesus. Respect your parents, pastors, and teachers. Respect your church leaders, but try their words and actions by the Scriptures and hang on to that part that is of God. The rest, humbly refuse. Everyone should follow this simple lifesaving method. Never judge truth by the number of people heading in that direction, even among God's remnant people. Remember the words of Jesus: "Broad is the way that leads to destruction, and there are many who go in by it. . . . Narrow is the gate and difficult is the way which leads to life, and there are few who find it" (Matthew 7:13, 14).

Recall the wildebeest crossing analogy so you don't ever forget to read the truth in God's Word. That alone will bring you life eternal.

Chapter 7

My First Unprepared Hike Up Mount Kenya

*As you walk up that straight and narrow mountain path, let your strength
and power come from God so you will make it to the top! You must be
prepared for the most difficult journey you have ever faced if you expect to succeed
eternally. If you want to win this all-out spiritual war, get your armor straight
from God's closet so that your victory is guaranteed! (Ephesians 6:10-13, PCRV).*

D uring our first year at Maxwell I discovered that one of the
highlights of the school year was climbing Mount Kenya.
At first it sounded intriguing, and I tried to mentally prepare myself to join the group. But by Christmas break my mentality had shifted. I knew I wasn't ready for this trek. It didn't help that
I had no equipment whatsoever, as I'd never climbed a mountain
before. Truth is, in the States I even hated walking to the local mall
and would rather do anything than hike.

Pastor Bert Williams, the music director at that time, led this
mountain expedition and had done so for several years, so he had
ample experience in leading novices such as me.

Our second year at Maxwell I decided it was time for me to
venture out and do something out of the ordinary. Each October
students and staff who are considering climbing Mount Kenya began
off-campus preparation hikes. So I joined up and began to prepare
physically for the big one.

The prep hikes, as we called them, weren't difficult for me, but
they became more and more challenging as each Sunday we hiked

a little farther than we had the week before. And of course, there were always a couple of students who'd jog the entire way instead of just walking. If I happened to be the staff leader that day, the joggers made actual "leading" difficult. I felt as though I needed to stay as close to the front of the group as possible, but at an elevation of 6,000 feet (1,800 meters) that wasn't an easy task! If it wasn't the student Blessed leading the pack one school year, it was Van and Simon the next. If that wasn't enough, I often had to struggle to stay up with Natsuki, a Japanese girl with a never-quit mentality. When those students graduated, even more young blood arrived on campus—kids such as Rei, Roger, and David. These guys came equipped with energizer batteries that never quit.

These wonderful students pushed me to the limit time and time again. Looking back, I often wonder why in the world we jogged on those prep hikes, because we never, ever jogged up Mount Kenya. Go figure! All my life I'd tried to stay physically fit. I'd kept active in sports. Sometimes as I puffed along on these prep hikes I could even believe I was still one of the guys. Then one day I got a slap-in-the-face reality check from Van Gulfan. It was on a Sabbath afternoon hike to the vertical bog area. Van, Simon, Natsuki, and I decided to run all the way back to met station, where we were acclimating for two days. We took off, and I was determined that this time around I wouldn't let them leave me in the dust.

I stayed right on the heels of one of them and, though perspiring greatly, ran all the way to the camp without stopping. I felt great in spite of the sweat because we'd made it in around 15 minutes, so I walked up to where the others had stopped to rest with my head justifiably swelling a bit. We were all breathing hard, but I gave them a big smile, and Van said, "Man, Pastor Curt, you are amazing!"

My head tilted a bit higher toward the sky as I thought, *Yes! I've still got it.* But then came the bomb that burst my bubble.

"Pastor Curt, you kept up with us the whole way. That's pretty amazing for a *guy your age!*"

There went any possibility of Van getting an A in my Bible class!

But that was a turning point in my life. I realized I had passed the point of no return when it came to being one of the guys. But in spite of that, I'd already decided that I actually enjoyed mountain climbing, so I was not going to hang up my backpack. At least not yet.

Finally came the day that everyone referred to as the Mount Kenya qualifier. This test would show if you had the willpower, the fortitude, the *purpose* to climb Mount Kenya. It determined if you were mentally and physically prepared to get to the top. This 20-mile (30-kilometer) hike started from the Maxwell campus and ended up back on campus. First we went along the road until we reached the saddle at Ngong Hills. From there we climbed to the fourth peak, ate a nice lunch, then headed back to campus.

The climb took us to almost 8,000 feet (2,400 meters) above sea level. The air is pretty thin up there, so it definitely was a challenge.

The way to the top wasn't so bad, but by the time I got back to the road my feet as were as sore as could be, and the soles of my feet felt as if they were on fire. With three miles (five kilometers) to go, every step on the tarmac burned like a hot bed of coals. My shoes offered no protection whatsoever against the pain. As I wearily dragged myself up a steep hill beyond a town called Kiserian, my supply of water ran out, and I began to crave something to drink. I felt as though I was dying of thirst. By the time the top of the hill was in sight, my body had stopped sweating, which told me that I was getting dehydrated.

Unfortunately, I had no money in my pocket, so even though I passed small shops that sold soda, I couldn't buy any. Finally, just before reaching the crest of the hill I knew I couldn't go on any further without liquid. My mouth felt like it was stuffed with cotton as I painfully walked to a nearby stand. Sure enough, I saw soda bottles inside the little store. I asked the owner if I could get a soda and pay him later, but he shook his head. I began to plead with him to give me a soda. I told him that if I didn't have one I would die of thirst right there on his step. I said that a dead man lying across the shop's doorstep would ruin any chance of him doing business. The man looked at me quizzically as I promised that I'd come back later that day and pay him 200 shillings—the cost of about 12 sodas.

At last he consented and gave me a bottle of orange Fanta. I didn't even care that it was warm as could be. The liquid and the sugar gave me the energy I needed to make it back to campus on my own two feet.

As I neared the last few yards toward the front entrance of Maxwell I saw a sight to behold! My kids were running down the road toward me with open arms and shouts of "Daddy!" while my wife stood smiling. I will never forget that sight as long as I live. It reminded me of Jesus.

How many times do we get weary in this world and feel like giving up? How often do we stumble to the ground wishing we could just go to sleep and not worry about struggling any longer? How many times does Jesus come running to encourage us and to lift us up and give us water from the everlasting well of His life? You remember Ellen White's vision of God's people traveling up a narrow path toward the city of God. "But soon some grew weary, and said the city was a great way off, and they expected to have entered it before. *Then Jesus would encourage them by raising His glorious right arm*" (*Early Writings,* p. 14; italics supplied). When you are feeling down and out and want to quit your fight against the foes of darkness, fix your eyes on Jesus and let Him carry you the rest of the way. He will carry you *and* your burdens. Jesus will never leave you to walk alone. If need be, He will provide you with the wings of eagles so you will soar through the sky of temptation, safely home into His arms.

During the weeks before we climbed Mount Kenya, Bert had lots of good advice for the hikers, especially those who had not climbed to the peak before. He told us what to expect at different points on the climb, what we needed to bring with us and what we should wear. Having never hiked at 10,000 to 16,200 feet (3,000 to 5,000 meters), I had no idea what the word "cold" meant. Bert said that we needed to make sure we had a warm sleeping bag. He talked about the importance of good hiking shoes or boots and how rough it would get if you wore the wrong kind of footwear or tried to break in new boots on the mountain. Looking back at that first year, I realize that if I'd listened more carefully, I would have had an easier time. If I had asked questions, I would have saved myself a lot of trouble. But I thought I knew what I was doing, and I thought I was prepared. More than a few surprises awaited me.

We started the climb about two weeks later. All our backpacks were packed with food, extra clothes, sleeping bags, and toilet paper. We were fortunate to be able to hike the first three hours without our backpacks as vehicles could take them up to Met Station—elevation 10,000 feet (3,000 meters). My backpack weighed about 70 pounds (26 kilograms), mostly because I planned to eat well on the mountain. I had the basic necessities—Big Franks and boxes of macaroni and cheese. I also brought a pretty thick sleeping bag that we already had from the States. It made my backpack quite bulky, but somehow the straps squeezed around it.

That first night at 10,000 feet (3,000 meters) found me freezing cold. I shivered and shook all night long, occasionally waking up and putting on more clothes, which seemed to make me even colder. "Some thick warm sleeping bag!" I told myself, almost angrily. Amazingly, once or twice I managed to drift off to sleep. About 2:00 a.m. I awoke having such a hard time breathing that I thought I was having a heart attack. I quickly sat up and tried to suck in some of the thin air, but it didn't help, and I began to panic. Finally I went outside, figuring it would be better if nobody saw me breathe my last. Surprisingly, as soon as I stepped out of the cabin I felt much better, and my breathing slowed to its normal pace. I had another problem, too. I needed to "go," but I was already so chilled that I couldn't imagine walking all the way down to the outhouse. So I stepped to the edge of the sidewalk facing down the hill. Now I knew why the grass was a lot greener there below the cabin than in most of the surrounding area. I did my part in promoting the growth of nature, then raced back to my now-icy sleeping bag.

I went through this routine a couple more times during the night, especially with the breathing difficulty, but finally the sun came up over the horizon. It was breathtaking, not only because the bitter cold refused to depart but also because of the clear blue sky and awe-inspiring surroundings.

We spent a relaxing, beautiful Sabbath day, including an afternoon hike to the vertical bog and back. The next morning we'd take off to the second camp, called MacKinder's, which is about 14,200 feet (4,300 meters) above sea level. This would prove to be a challenging hike, especially through the bog. The nature of a bog is to have water here and there, and this year of my first climb was no exception. I'd decided to wear my fairly new boots, which I'd purchased on Biashara Street at a local shoe store. They served me well until we got to the bog, when I think my new boots found every waterhole there was. By the time I made it to the next camp my wet feet were completely numb. Also, part of one sole had started to come undone, giving me a nice airhole so my feet could breathe.

Somehow I struggled to the camp, excited that I'd made it to another milestone. The next morning would hopefully take us to the top, and then we would begin the trek back to the first station. It was cold at MacKinder's Camp, especially after the sun went down, but the beauty made all the suffering worthwhile. Through the clear air we could see the jagged top of Mount Kenya as well as the scree slope. That slippery slope would prove to be the greatest challenge in my mind, especially during the middle of the night. I had a terrible headache (probably from the altitude) the whole time at MacKinder's, which made it difficult to eat anything or even drink water. I knew Bert had emphasized the importance of drinking water even when you weren't thirsty, so I tried to sip some here and there, but it was tough, as my stomach wanted to reject almost everything.

That evening we tried to get to sleep early, but it was impossible for me. Reason number one was that there were 25 other people in the same room. Second, five of them snored quite loudly, and I am a light sleeper. So most of the night I lay on my back staring into the darkness and wondering why in the world I would give up my nice bed back home for this! My alarm went off about 2:00 a.m., and I got up and made lots of noise, mostly to get even with those who'd kept me awake the whole night. Soon everyone was ready to go, and some even tried to get some food down. I had a couple of

Nutri-Grain bars, which I swallowed with great difficulty, and then at 3:00 a.m. we took off.

To describe the beauty of the night at 14,200 feet (4,300 meters) is virtually impossible. With no light pollution, millions of twinkling stars covered the sky. It was astounding. We followed Bert, tramping along single file, until gradually the stronger ones began pulling ahead of the others. Within about 45 minutes we started up the scree slope. It was so steep that we had to zigzag all the way to its top. It was bitterly cold. The wind bit through my down-filled Michigan winter coat as though it were no heavier than a cotton T-shirt. The staff carried radios and used them often, as many times it was difficult to see which way we should go. How encouraging it was to radio Bert or Arne to signal with their flashlight so we could see the right direction to turn. Just to see that small light beaming down the mountain warmed our hearts as much as the sun coming up in the east. It showed us that we weren't alone, that others had gone ahead of us and knew the way. Without help from those above, surely some of us would have gone the wrong direction and gotten lost.

What an apt parallel to our walk with Christ. Through inspiration David tells us that God's "word is a lamp unto my feet, and a light unto my path" (Psalm 119:105, KJV). We sometimes grow weary in our Christian walk and may lose our way. Darkness presses around us, trying to shut out the light from God. When that happens, we can get out our radios (called prayer) and contact Headquarters! Then we must go to the Word of God and meekly learn at Jesus' feet.

The Word is the flashlight that will illuminate our path, and if we follow it, there's nothing Satan can do to stop us. Follow God's light, and your steps will be sure. The Scriptures are the only thing that Satan cannot argue with, and its promises are ours for the taking! God put His promises in the Bible for us to learn from them and use them to our advantage in every situation. That's how Jesus succeeded against the devil, and that's exactly how you and I can overcome Satan. If you ever find yourself in darkness and can't seem to press forward, stop where you are, pray, then break out God's Word until the light beams down from above. Follow that light. It will lead you to Jesus, no matter how biting cold the winds of temptation.

At last we all made it to the top of the scree slope. Only another 500 feet (150 meters) to the summit! The air was extremely thin, and I walked very slowly, because my Nutri-Grain bars were trying to come up and join me. It felt as if someone were blowing bubbles in my stomach, but I pressed on, even trying my best to encourage the students along the way. Then we saw the sun coming up in the east, and the sight of it was wonderful! Our spirits lifted with the darkness as the clear, golden sunshine streamed into our beings. We somehow knew at that point that we were going to make it.

The path took us higher and higher through a rather rocky area, and a couple of times I looked down over the sides. As I was afraid of heights, it made me angry. I couldn't believe that we were taking students through this dangerous area without ropes. A couple of times I was pretty mentally challenged (all right, scared—are you happy?), but I found that keeping my eyes on the ground by my feet and not looking down helped me tremendously. In later years I gave the same advice to some girls who fearfully clung to the side of the rock walls and refused to go any farther. Hand in hand, we made it to the top by looking down at our steps and nowhere else.

Finally we saw the top and climbed that last rocky crag, where we were met with cheers from those tough enough to stand there braving the cold. It was exhilarating to feel the strong wind and to take in the beautiful morning. A couple of us even tried to do hand-stands to celebrate the victory over this mountain.

Little did I realize that the most difficult part of this climb was going down.

We didn't stay long on the summit, and by the time I reached the scree slope the holes in my boots had almost doubled in size. My feet were cold, and not only that, the steep downward angle caused my toes to press tightly against the front of the shoes, which, of course, gave me terrible blisters. After stopping and picking up my backpack, I finally headed back down to met station. I was assigned to the rear of the group with Dana Pottle and one of the student missionaries. We slowly plodded along, as each step I took was very painful. I'm not sure which was worse, the pain in my cold, wet feet, the muscle soreness in my legs, or my shoulders, where the straps from the backpack unmercifully pulled and dug into my flesh.

Eventually we made it back to the vertical bog area, which was even spongier than it had been on our way up. If memory serves me correctly, rain was falling as we entered this stage of our journey, and that made it even worse. In the bog you consistently step down over knolls of grass or up over rocks. You can imagine the pressure this put on your muscles and knees. Remember, too, that we were carrying about 50 pounds (20 kilograms) on our backs. I don't recall how many times I stepped into water and mudholes, but it was a *lot*, and my feet were a mess. If it wasn't me plunging into another hole, then it was Dana or the student missionary, and by the time we got through the bog we were a sight to behold. Now is when mental toughness grew vital to our finishing the course. All muscle strength was long gone, so to move forward you had to will your leg to take a step. My legs felt so numb that I nearly had to pick them up one at a time and throw them forward. It was a classic battle of the will against the elements of nature.

Nearing the tree line we found that most of the path had turned to mud. What a nightmare! At one point I was in the lead when I heard a kind of "Ohhh" behind me and turned to see if someone had fallen. No one had fallen, but I saw Dana burst through the trees in a dead run, out of control, unable to stop her downward flight as the result of her momentum. I wish I'd had a camera, for it was both incredible and entertaining. I fully expected her to hit the ground any moment, but, unbelievably, she held her feet and grabbed at passing bushes and finally came to a stop just a couple of feet from me. I couldn't believe she didn't fall and fall hard. It took some athleticism and serious focus for her to maintain control when all seemed lost, especially because of the long, exhausting hike we'd already done that day. I had a good laugh as she and I stood there wishing for hot showers and some warm food.

We finally reached the last section in the path to met station. I

couldn't swear it was true, but we were all quite certain that someone had added 12 new turns! It seemed to take forever to reach the
camp, but reach it we finally did. I felt a little disappointed that no
one was there to cheer our arrival. Of course, if they'd felt the way
I did at that point, I suspect they were soaking their feet or were
on their cots, snoring. What a trip! As I look back on that first
Mount Kenya climb, I realize that I was about as prepared as a fish
out of water. I was wearing terrible, cheap shoes, and they made
my life miserable. My sleeping bag was almost useless against the
cold. It worked well only as an invitation for the cold air to come
in and join me. My backpack was too heavy, and I brought way
too many clothes. I'd borrowed the backpack, and didn't realize
the importance of a frame to take some of the weight off my shoulders. If only I had paid more attention to our guide, I wouldn't
have stressed so much when I couldn't breathe well that first night.
He had warned us that at first we might have trouble breathing on
the mountain.

When our family went on furlough the following summer, I
bought everything I needed to climb that mountain again. I spared
no expense because I knew that getting the best would make the
next trip much easier and much more enjoyable. I bought one pair
of hiking shoes and another pair of Gortex-lined boots to keep out
the water. I bought a nice backpack with an external frame, and the
difference was awesome. I bought lightweight packets of nutritious
food—easy to pack and carry, unlike my heavy cans of Big Franks.
I also bought a sleeping bag made for use in *really* cold weather, and
it's kept me toasty warm up on the mountain ever after. Last but not
at all the least, I decided to listen more carefully to the guide. He had
made the climb a few times before, and he knew what to expect.

One of the most amazing insights I had on Mount Kenya was
how similar climbing a mountain is to my spiritual walk with Jesus.
Sometimes the way is tremendously difficult, but as long as you're
traveling upward with Jesus as your guide you will find peace and
tranquillity all along the way. God never promised a rose garden if
you sacrifice your life to Him, but He did promise to be with you

all the rest of your life! No matter what the condition of the pathway, you will never travel alone. And when the going gets tough, Jesus will carry you on His massive shoulders.

Of course, it's vital that you be prepared for this life hike. This is no regular battle we fight. To survive, you must be wearing the full armor of God. Spare no expense, my friend! Buy top-of-the-line truth-filled mountain-tested pants. If you wish to stay healthy, cover your upper body with the righteousness of Jesus. Your feet must be concealed with the best possible gospel-of-peace shoes that there are on the market. This mountain is so great and terrible that you must take the shield of faith to protect you when nasty tempting winds breathe down your neck. Christ's shield will be to you as a warm fireplace in a cozy den at home. Cover your head with the helmet of salvation, and never forget that the Word of God is your light. It will help you see the way until the *Son* rises with healing in His wings (see Malachi 4:2). Above all, take your Guide's hand and trust Him implicitly all along the way. Leave all your stress and worry to Him. He's been to the top before and knows just what it takes to get there safely.

Chapter 8

Paul's Fight Against the Prince of Darkness

*Don't think that we spiritually wrestle with other human beings like
ourselves! We are fighting against Satan and his angels, who rule this dark
world, and unlike you and me, they have supernatural power. Because we
are weak, we must surrender our lives and decisions to the God of heaven,
then through the power of prayer we can command Satan to leave us. He has no choice
but to go, because God is in our midst! (Ephesians 6:12, PCRV; James 4:7, PCRV).*

What you are about to read is not for the faint of heart. *If
you are a young person, I strongly encourage you to have Mom
or Dad read this story first, and let them decide whether it is ap-
propriate for you.* This story could cause many feelings to course
through your blood—feelings of amazement, fear, sadness, and joy.
More than anything else, I pray that after you read about this young
man's incredible experience against the powers of darkness, you will
experience a feeling of hope that you've never felt before! Of
course, I cannot share this student's real name, because I want to
protect his privacy. So I am going to call him Paul.

Paul grew up in a well-respected Seventh-day Adventist home.
As a young boy he went to school just like everybody else his age.
And it was at school that he faced a terrible situation that no boy or
girl should ever have to deal with. A teacher sexually molested him
more than once. As is often the case, Paul didn't know where to
turn or even if there was anyone who could help him. So instead of
telling a trusted adult what had happened, he kept all the fear, anger,

103

and even shame bottled up inside. As usually happens, the more he kept things bottled up, the angrier he became, until it rose to a boiling point. Even though he still didn't trust anyone, he began to search for someone to help him. It was too much pain and anguish for a young boy to carry in his heart.

As a pastor and teacher I often counsel students. I am increasingly amazed at how many have been sexually molested or abused in some way, and yet have never been able to share their burden. Maybe *you* are one of those kids who have kept things bottled up inside. If so, let me assure you that Jesus loves you and knows that what happened was not your fault. Next, if you don't share your outrage with someone, sooner or later your pain will reveal itself—often in ugly, destructive ways. Then your life only gets worse. Third, if you don't share with someone you can trust, Satan will be waiting around the corner to give you *his* kind of help. Last, you don't have to face this on your own. Please tell someone you can trust (pastor, teacher, or parent). Believe it or not, sharing will lessen the burden. And I assure you that God can take your pain and heartache away.

Paul chose not to trust family members or others by telling them what had happened. Perhaps he didn't think that he could, or maybe he just couldn't find the words. Tragically, because he was already hurting, the devil was able to ensnare him even further into his web of lies and deception. It wasn't long before Satan took advantage of the situation and impressed one of Paul's friends to encourage him to visit a witch doctor. The friend told him that the witch doctor would be able to help. And being one of the devil's right-hand men, the witch doctor directed Paul to a "nice" group of young men. They called themselves the Brotherhood, and they offered friendship and lifelong support. It seemed to Paul just what he was looking for.

Paul's need was so great that he ignored the red flag raised by their motto: *Live by the gun, die by the gun.* It's interesting that this sounds a lot like something Jesus told Peter: "Put your sword in its place, for all who take the sword will perish by the sword" (Matthew 26:52).

The Brotherhood of young men was nothing more than Satan worshippers. All their time was spent planning revenge on those who hurt them. It wasn't beyond the Brotherhood to beat up, rape, and even murder anyone who crossed them. But they accepted Paul into their group, and he literally signed his life over to Satan, pledging himself to be a part of the satanic brotherhood family until the day he died.

Paul knew exactly what this meant. It was a conscious decision to reject God and a personal vow to serve Satan. And Paul quickly rose to leadership in the Brotherhood, proving himself a capable, decisive leader.

Yet something else was going on despite Paul's decision to follow Satan. Someone else was watching him, and that Someone was Jesus Christ, the God of heaven. I want to point out this very important fact. When God makes up His mind that it's time that our circumstances change, the forces of evil had better look out! God loved Paul with all His heart and somewhere deep down inside that young man God saw the pain of a broken heart lost in Satan's world. God saw someone who was longing to be found.

Operation Save Paul began to move forward. God started to move His mighty hand of power over Paul's life, and it wasn't long before Mom and Dad came home with great news. They had made arrangements for Paul to attend a Christian school called Maxwell Adventist Academy near the town of Ongata Rongai.

As you can imagine, the young men in the Brotherhood were angry about this. The leaders went to Paul ranting and raving that he could not attend a Christian school because the master (Satan) refused to allow his children to be placed where God's influence could affect them.

Paul adamantly assured them that he would remain true to his pledge. He told them that it wasn't *his* choice to attend this school. During the school's open weekends he'd still meet with the Brotherhood so their plans for revenge could still go on as usual. And for a time Paul kept his promise. He didn't want to go to MAA anyway, but praise the Lord, his parents gave him no choice.

So like it or not, Paul joined the student body of Maxwell Academy. He went to his classes, he hung out with guys in the dorm, and he sat through daily worships and weekend church services. Affecting every good experience was the heavy burden he still carried on his heart. But because the Holy Spirit was working mightily on him, Paul finally opened up to a staff member, Debbie Herold. She counseled and prayed with him often, and did her best to help him survive his struggles. Again and again she urged Paul to take the hand of the One who could save him from this torture. Of course, Satan didn't want to let him go, and at different times Paul was possessed by a demon. Then Debbie would pray for him, imploring God to save him from the evil one. Gradually Paul began to respond to the Holy Spirit, and God's plan for Paul moved steadily forward.

The school year ended . . . the next school year began. As season followed season Paul gradually realized that the sort of life he had with the satanic cult didn't make him happy. At the same time the pain of his past often resurfaced, and with it the anger. Besides that, he would soon lose the friendly support of the Herold family, for they were moving away. Paul decided to find someone else he could trust. Surely God led in his search, for he found Dana Pottle.

It was during the senior class trip to the coast that Paul, led by the Spirit of God, opened up to Dana. She realized that God had opened a door for her to plant even more seeds in Paul's heart, and she took the challenge seriously. She never passed up an opportunity to talk to Paul, leading him step by step to Jesus and the Scriptures. Time after time Dana prayed with Paul, asking God to intervene in his life and to help him have the strength to leave the Brotherhood for good. But Satan wasn't about to let that happen! Word might get out to others in his grasp that there was a way to escape the horrors of his evil hand.

During the latter part of that school year demons tried to possess Paul, torturing his mind and controlling his body. Sometimes Paul felt life itself being squeezed out of him. In desperation he'd call for Dana, who would pray for him, imploring God to protect him from the demons and to spare his life. And each time God would move His all-powerful hand and turn the tide in Paul's eternal favor, giving him another opportunity to commit his life to the great Life-giver.

It was during one of these times that I was called to the church. I found Paul lying on the floor of the church balcony looking as if he was in his final moments of life. We prayed a couple of times for Paul, who lay there helpless. His eyes were a blank stare. He seemed drained of energy. He couldn't even speak audibly. It took some time before Paul was able to push himself up on his hands and knees, then finally get up off the floor and leave the church. Dana and I were amazed at the patience and long-suffering of God.

I just love that about God! Even in spite of our past sins, God still does everything possible to draw us into His loving arms. God doesn't just see a sinner in you or me. He sees *His* child, whom He loves with all His forgiving heart. Listen to the beautiful character-revealing words found in Psalm 103:8-14. "The Lord is merciful and gracious, slow to anger, and abounding in mercy. He will not always strive with us, nor will He keep His anger forever. He has not dealt with us according to our sins, nor punished us according to our iniquities. For as the heavens are high above the earth, so great is His mercy toward those who fear Him; as far as the east is from the west, so far has He removed our transgressions from us. As a father pities his children, so the Lord pities those who fear Him. For He knows our frame; He remembers that we are dust."

Isn't that just like God? Jesus knows we are sinners, but He has an unlimited capability to see beyond the ugliness and into the heart that desires a loving Savior, a heart that only He can make perfect when we truly surrender to Him.

You might wonder why God allowed Paul to be harassed by demons. It was because of Paul's connections with the Brotherhood that Satan was allowed to remain in his life. Paul refused to sever his relationship with them, and again and again that friendship opened the door to demons. *"No one can serve two masters; for either he will hate the one and love the other, or else he will be loyal to the one and despise the other"* (Matthew 6:24). Don't ever fool yourself into thinking you can hang on to both the world and God. Each is completely contrary to the other, and if you keep your feet in both worlds, you are as lost as if you were a demon worshipper. God cannot share even a small part of you with Satan, because that evil seed will soon sprout into a choking vine that will smother the Life-giver out of you.

One night Paul awoke and immediately felt a demon presence there in his dorm room. Fear filled his heart, and his mind raced as he tried to think what to do. Then suddenly he remembered what he'd been told by Dana and others: "Call on Jesus to fight for you." He would do it!

"In Jesus' name, leave me alone!" he commanded, his voice quivering with fear.

"I'll leave for now," the demon retorted, "but I'll be back."

Little did Paul realize that he was in for a long fight for his life. As the school year neared its close, Dana felt impressed that Paul needed to give his life completely to Christ through baptism. He needed to sign his life *back* over to God. When a person signs his or her life back to God, Satan's contract is no longer valid. Dana shared her convictions with Paul, and through the Holy Spirit he decided that he would make that public commitment. A couple of weeks before the scheduled baptism Paul dreamed that Satan was standing next to him. "Do you choose Him [Jesus] or me?" Satan asked.

"I choose Him!" Paul said. At that Satan grabbed him and held him over a fire.

Helpless to resist, Paul cried out, "Jesus, save me!" At that moment Paul awoke safely in his dorm room while peace filled his heart.

It seemed a long wait to me, but Paul was finally baptized near the end of the year. Both Dana and I felt that maybe this would be the turning point in his life. We felt that through baptism Paul might forever be released from Satan's icy grip, but we couldn't have been more wrong. After graduation weekend Paul moved back home and unfortunately continued seeing his old "friends." They happily greeted him and acted as if having him back were renewing old times, but more than once he was attacked and beaten unconscious by these satanic worshippers. He would awaken bruised and bleeding but thankfully still alive. Many times, day and night, Dana or I would feel impressed to pray for Paul. Of course we always did, unsure of what was happening in his life. In vain we tried to convince Paul that he must stop his friendship with the Brotherhood; our words seemed to fall on deaf ears.

On one occasion Paul was in a car with three or four of these guys traveling down a main road in Nairobi when suddenly Paul heard a voice command, *Get out of the car!*

Paul jumped out at the next stop sign and ran down a side street as fast as he could. He found out later that these men were taking him to a warehouse to kill him.

Later that year Paul called Dana and told her that one of his good friends had committed suicide and that he had promised to go to the funeral. Dana called me and asked what I thought about that. After some discussion I felt that he should be able to go without fear from Satan or his friends, as God would protect him.

Later Dana called me again. After discussing new facts Paul had given her, we both felt strongly that this could be a setup and that he should not go under any circumstances. Once again God had intervened. Later it was discovered that the funeral was going to be a celebration that would climax with the murder of Paul.

Then a hit was put out on his life, but even that was to no avail. God was on hand to save him. Despite the fact that these hired hit men had never failed on a contract to destroy a life, they were unable to kill Paul.

Another time Dana and Paul were in a restaurant in deep spiritual discussion when Paul looked over at another table and saw two of the highest members in the Brotherhood staring intently at him. Paul was scared stiff, and quietly explained to Dana his sudden fear for his life. He was sure they were there to kill him. Dana prayed that God would protect them, and God sent His angels to keep Paul and Dana safe.

Satan was getting desperate, for he hates to lose even one soul to

Christ, his enemy. The Brotherhood came up with what they thought was a foolproof plan to bring Paul down. They raped and later killed a young woman, framing Paul for the crime. They actually gave false testimony to the police, hoping that Paul would be arrested and executed, but again it came to nothing. When God stands up and says, "Enough is enough; this far you may come but no farther," neither Satan nor any of his host can put one toenail over that line.

Dana and I talked and prayed much about Paul and about our dismay at how he just didn't seem to get it. Neither of us could believe that after all that had happened, especially all the times God had intervened to save him from certain death, Paul *still* hung on to these supposed friends. On more than one occasion we mentioned that sooner or later Paul would face a final showdown. We fully believe that had it not been for intercessory prayer he wouldn't be alive today. When God impresses you to pray for someone, don't delay for even a moment. You might be freeing the hand of God to save a precious soul. *With God all things are possible.*

I picture it kind of like this. A young man makes a choice to serve self instead of God. He consciously says, "God, I won't have You reign over me, so leave me alone!" God, of course, respects his right to choose whom he wishes to serve. Satan gloats as he takes control of that young man's life and is happy that God doesn't stop him. But our loving God impresses one of *His* children to pray for that young man, and when they do He gets involved through the power of the Holy Spirit.

Satan screams his displeasure, shouting out, "Hey, God, wait a minute. He chose me! You respect freedom of choice, so leave him alone."

God calmly retorts to His archenemy, "Satan, do you see my servant over there? She is praying for Me to get involved, and I am answering her intercessory prayer for that young man. I have *every* right to be here, so you just move on."

Don't ever lose hope and assume that someone you love will never surrender to Jesus Christ. As long as you pray there's *always* hope, even when a person is willingly serving in the kingdom of

Satan. Zechariah 3:2 forcefully reminds us of God's power to save. "And the Lord said to Satan, 'The Lord rebuke you, Satan! The Lord who has chosen Jerusalem rebuke you! Is this not a brand plucked from the fire?'"

Whether you see no results for days, months, or even years, never give up interceding for that friend or loved one, for *nothing* is impossible for our God, who has all power to save every soul. Hebrews 7:25 reminds us that Jesus lives to intercede for us, and He would have us take part in that intercession for others, especially if they refuse to come to Jesus themselves.

The final unforgettable showdown for Paul's life came during Mother's Day weekend. I will never forget that day as long as I live. I had just given a sermon based upon mothers, and I was sitting in my home office thinking about my mom. Tears had fallen down my cheeks, as I wished my mom were still alive so that I could spend time with her. Suddenly my daughter Stephanie rushed into my office, out of breath. "Aunt Dana called and said for you to come down to the hostel right away!" she gasped. "Hurry!"

I quickly wiped my eyes and raced out the door, unsure of what was going on but somehow feeling that Paul was involved. Dana met me, a look of desperation and fear on her face.

"I was just on the phone with Paul, and the line went dead. I think he's in trouble," Dana said as we sat down on the couch in her living room. "He'd called and asked me to pray for him; then suddenly I heard him scream, and the line went dead."

Dana was distraught. She had no idea where Paul had been when he called, and she didn't know what to do. I too felt a helpless apprehension for Paul's safety and thought of the only help we could possibly offer.

"Let's pray, Curt," she said. "I think we need to pray." So without having any clue what had happened to Paul, we knelt down by the couch and prayed. Dana went first, begging God for Paul's safety; then I prayed. I don't recall our exact words, but it was something like this:

"Dear God, we come to You because we feel Paul is in danger

of some sort, but we don't know what it is. Please keep him safe and rescue him from danger. We know that he has made many bad choices. We know that he has hung on to those friends of his, but we implore You to intervene despite his bad choices and spare his life. Open his eyes to see that he must make changes and that he must completely follow You. God, we believe that You haven't brought Paul this far only to let Satan take his life now. Save him, Lord. Please spare his life again."

After we each prayed aloud we remained kneeling, silently lifting our requests to God. Somehow we both felt that the time was now for Paul to decide once and for all. After praying silently for a while, Dana asked me how I felt. "I think we need to pray aloud again," I told her.

"I have the same feeling," she said. "We *must* keep on praying for him."

We felt that whatever was going on, things were getting more desperate. So again we prayed, fervently pleading with God to step in and save Paul's life.

Dana's eloquent prayer came from her heart. She had spent so much time with Paul. She could not let Satan have him. Then I began to plead with God, but as I spoke my body began to shake as if I were standing at the South Pole with no clothes on. I didn't feel cold, but I had no control over the shaking and soon recognized that another power was in the living room with us and it was not happy with our prayer meeting.

"Dear Father in heaven," I began, "I can feel the presence of evil angels in this room. I know that they are desperately trying to stop us from praying. Father, my body is shaking because Satan's angels are pressing in on us, but I have full confidence that we are being protected by Your angels whom You have sent here. Dear God, drive the evil angels away so that Your mighty hand might move in Paul's behalf," I implored Him. "Drive them away from us, and save Paul."

When I finished, I opened my eyes and looked at Dana. "I'm feeling a sense of coldness around my body, too," she said. We felt that we must keep praying, and prayed even more fervently than before. After this second prayer God intervened by driving the evil angels away, and the shaking and coldness disappeared. Not once did either of us feel any sense of fear. We knew that God was in that room and that we were sheltered under His arms of strength and love. We felt such humility that God counted us worthy to protect under such adverse circumstances.

After praying a third time, we remained on our knees, silently pleading with God. Finally after one last prayer time we both agreed that we were released from praying any further. We got up and sat on the couch, almost disbelieving what had just happened. I remember feeling a sense of deep humility that God had responded to our prayers. Dana and I talked about the possibility that Paul might have died but that God had saved him eternally. Whether his life had been saved or not, we strongly believed that God had accomplished His lifesaving grace in Paul's life.

I walked back home in a sort of daze, wondering if Paul was alive or dead and wishing I could know what had happened. Two days passed before we learned the most amazing story I've ever heard. If I hadn't been part of it, I might not believe it myself.

The following Monday Dana was able to reach Paul on the phone, and she set up a meeting with him. We were so relieved that he was alive. He looked OK, but kind of glum. We started our visit with prayer, and then told Paul that we knew that something terrible had happened on Sabbath afternoon, and we wanted to know what it was so we could glorify God.

His eyes filled with fear, and he immediately hung his head. "I'm afraid to tell you," he said quietly.

"Paul, are you afraid that someone will hurt you if you tell us?" Dana asked.

He didn't say much, but continued to shake his head, implying that he *couldn't* tell us. We prayed again, asking God to give Paul the strength to share what had happened. We told him that we knew that his life had been in terrible danger and that we had prayed earnestly for his life to be saved. We shared with him how we had felt evil angels in Dana's living room and how they had tried to stop us from praying. At that, he looked up incredulously. I think he hardly dared to believe our experience. Again I appealed to him to let God be glorified by sharing the details with us. Gradually confidence replaced fear as we assured him that God had saved his life and that He would *not* let him be killed by the devil now. At last Paul said that he would tell us.

After church Paul had gone to the home of some friends to hang out. The teens were all sitting in the living room talking and visiting when Paul looked across the room and saw a couple of men from the Brotherhood. The strange thing was that he hadn't noticed them before that point. Paul's heart pounded. *When had they come in? What did they want?* His mouth felt lined with dust as he looked at the evil intent in their faces.

Panicked, he couldn't think what to do next. But when he saw a demon coming toward him from the other side of the room he jumped up and raced to the bedroom. That's when he picked up the phone and called Dana. As he choked out the words for her to pray for him, he turned around and saw the demon come into the room. The demon grabbed him and began to strangle him. That's when he screamed and the phone went dead.

The hand of Satan's angel held Paul in the grip of death, yet two or three times he was able to escape, and ran to the window to jump out. Each time the demon caught him, his fingers crushing Paul's throat. This must have been about the first time we prayed—some 30 miles (50 kilometers) away. Maybe God sent an angel to release the demon's hold to allow Paul to escape for short periods of time.

By now Paul felt himself about to pass out from lack of oxygen. Just then his gaze drifted to the bedroom doorway, and he saw another demon walk into the room. This was not the usual demon that harassed him, but a different one. Paul told us that seeing it, he felt more terror than he'd ever had in his life, more even than feeling his life strangled away by the first demon. There was something odd about this demon, Paul said. The form of a snake rose up from behind his head. At that I caught my breath, and goose bumps covered my body.

"Paul, do you realize that that demon was probably none other than Satan himself coming to finish the job?" I asked with both excitement and incredulity. Paul's head dropped, shaking back and forth in amazement. Dana and I sat stunned, almost in disbelief.

Paul said that second demon grabbed him by the throat and began to strangle him. At that point he knew that his life was over. It was most likely then that Satan sent some of his forces to interrupt our prayer meeting, and it is most likely that this was the time we felt the greatest urge to pray as never before.

Just as Paul felt himself on the edge of consciousness his mind went to Jesus for the first time throughout this encounter. So far through this terrible event God had intervened, graciously sparing his life. But He knew that He could save Paul only if Paul wanted to be saved. Our prayers kept him alive long enough to see his folly and to give him one last chance before his choices forever sealed his fate.

Darkness closing in on him, his larynx crushed by strong fingers, Paul couldn't speak. But mentally he cried out three words, and that prayer saved his life.

"Jesus, save me!"

That was all, but it was enough. Just like Peter of old who was sinking beneath the waves of the Sea of Galilee, Paul cried out to God. In a heartbeat he was released and sank to the floor. He sat for a moment in silence. Satan and the demons were gone, and he felt peace.

He got up and walked back into the living room, where his friends still sat talking. When they saw him come through the hallway, they jumped up, puzzled and excited.

"How'd you do that?" they asked.

"How did I do what?"

"You were just sitting here with us, and then all of a sudden you came walking in from the back bedroom," they responded, nervously looking around the room.

It seems obvious that while Satan was in the back room trying to murder Paul, one of his demons had taken on Paul's appearance and sat visiting with the friends and relatives.

Dana and I sat dumbfounded, alternately speechless and praising the good Lord for what He had done for Paul and for us.

Paul's life was never the same. At last he completely surrendered his life to God. He and Dana spoke through e-mail a number of times, and I learned that he was giving Bible studies to other young people like himself and that he remained headed in the right direction.

I learned a lot from Paul's story and this final climatic experience. First is that no matter how far you slip into self and this world, God can still rescue you. I also learned that as Job 38:11 implies, God is still in control even of Satan, and He will draw the line beyond which Satan cannot go. Third, I now understand that God's love is much greater than Satan's hatred. Last, I learned that *the prayer of faith will save the sick,* whether it is physical sickness or spiritual sickness. God implores all of us, "Pray for one another, that you may be healed. The effective, fervent prayer of a righteous [man or woman or child] avails much" (James 5:16). I know that I am not righteous, but when you and I allow Jesus to come into our hearts and we pray with faith in Him, His righteousness comes out in us, and that's all that counts.

Remember always that when the going gets tough, just *PUSH.* I don't know who said it first, but I love the concept: **Pray Until Something Happens.** We fight against not human beings but against Satan and all his forces, and we need to get God involved immediately.

In an inspired book called *In Heavenly Places,* God reveals to us what prayer does to the kingdom of darkness. "If Satan sees that he is in danger of losing one soul, he will exert himself to the utmost to keep that one. And when the individual is aroused to his danger, and, with distress and fervor, looks to Jesus for strength, Satan fears that he will lose a captive, and he calls a reinforcement of his angels to hedge in the poor soul, and form a wall of darkness around him, that heaven's light may not reach him.

"But if the one in danger perseveres, and in his helplessness casts himself upon the merits of the blood of Christ, our Savior listens to the earnest prayer of faith, and sends a reinforcement of those angels that excel in strength to deliver him. Satan cannot endure to have his powerful rival appealed to, for he fears and trembles before His strength and majesty. At the sound of fervent prayer, Satan's whole host trembles. . . . And when angels, all-powerful, clothed with the armory of heaven, come to the help of the fainting, pursued soul, Satan and his host fall back. . . . The great Commander in heaven and earth has limited Satan's power" (p. 253).

When you are at the bottom of the barrel . . .

When you have nothing else left . . .

When you feel that there's no way out . . .

You can *always, always* pray! *You always have Jesus Christ!* Don't ever forget it.

Chapter 9

A Principal, a Pastor, and One Python

People often play with sin as if it's harmless. They feel that any time they choose they can put sin away in a cage where it will not escape. I tell you the truth, sin cannot be caged in your life! It will infiltrate your mind and body until it completely destroys you in the end! (Proverbs 14:12, PCRV).

One of my favorite spare-time activities is to identify birds, otherwise known as birding. When you live in one of the best birding places in the world it's difficult to pass up any opportunity, and some of the birds in Kenya are simply breathtaking. I will never forget the gorgeous turacos. They are most beautiful when they fly, and the ones I saw generate a rich red color when they fly that you don't see when their wings are folded. This red contrasts nicely with the beautiful green of most of their feathers. One bird we watched for about two hours one morning at Lake Baringo took my breath away. It was a northern red bishop—the most beautiful bird I've ever seen. Beneath the morning sun's rays, its brilliant red feathers radiantly shine against jet black portions of its body. It is one of the greatest pieces of God's handiwork in the world.

Back before I entered the birding world, one Sabbath afternoon my in-laws decided to take my wife and me with them on a birding expedition around Berrien Springs, Michigan. When Kim told me of their plans, I looked at her to see if she was serious. She was, and I thought to myself, *OK, how many times can we stare at a robin, a blue jay, or a cardinal?* That was the extent of my birding ability, and

I could see those birds without leaving my backyard. I reluctantly went along with Kim and her parents and was amazed at how many different birds there were right around us. By the third time out I was hooked, and I've never looked back. When I got to Kenya and saw the 1,200 different species listed in the country's bird book, I figured we'd entered birding heaven. So whenever an opportunity came to grab some binoculars and an East African bird book, I took it without so much as a second thought.

One day the principal, Arne Nielsen, called and asked if I wanted to head to the game park the next day and do some birding. My schedule didn't look overly exciting, so I quickly agreed. Early the next day we headed to the Nairobi Game Park, intent on relaxing for the morning with the birds and animals.

Things went quite well. We saw some good birds and got some decent pictures, and I was able to add a few new birds to my life list. That's always a good thing and makes for a good feeling at the end of the day. Then about 10:00 a.m., as we drove toward a place called Kingfisher Point, we both noticed a small white car just sitting. In the game park if you see a car stopped longer than the norm you figure they're watching an interesting animal, so we ventured in that direction. However, just before we came close enough to see what was going on, the car pulled out and left without a glance in our direction. Usually those who have seen a special animal let passersby know, so we figured they hadn't seen anything interesting. All the same, we decided to stop and take a look around. Arne thought that maybe they'd been watching a cheetah, as the cats had been seen around there before. So we got out our binoculars and checked out the area. No cheetah. Nothing. We'd been sitting just a few moments, near the exact spot the other vehicle had been, when Arne glanced out his window and said, "Hey, look over here!"

I leaned over and looked out the window to where he was pointing. There on the ground not 10 feet (three meters) away was a snake, and it was *big*. In fact, it was much bigger than most other snakes I'd seen up close.

One thing I have to point out before finishing this story is that catching snakes is very similar to catching fish. I don't know why it happens, but it does. Fish always look bigger than they really are, especially when they escape off a person's line. Hence the fish stories: "Man, you should have seen the one that got away. It was *this* big!" And the speaker's hands are held about three feet apart even though the fish was actually just a six-and-one-half-inch (16.5-centimeter) sunfish. Well, there's something about seeing a snake that brings out the best in us when relating the actual size of the thing.

I'm telling you that this snake outside Arne's window looked at least 10 feet (three meters) long and was about as big around as my calf. It was a southern African rock python, and I could see that it was truly a man-eater—but more about that later. Arne looked down at the snake. I looked at Arne. He looked at me as I looked at the snake. Almost simultaneously we looked up the road, then back down the road. Not a car was in sight.

Are you thinking what I'm thinking?
Are you thinking what I'm thinking?

No words were spoken, but we both knew what we wanted to do. One thing about both of us is that we are always looking for an adventure, especially when it comes to nature. We had to be careful, though, because we could get thrown out of the park for getting out of our car. Arne said something like "Well, what do you think we should do?" I knew very well that the lighting duing that time of day wasn't very good for taking pictures, so I was sure that he wasn't talking about photography.

I responded without a moment's hesitation. "Let's catch it!"
"But how?"

I was expecting that question and already had the answer. "I'll grab it by the tail end and wear it out a bit," I said confidently. "Then you find a big stick, pin its head down, and then grab it behind the head."

Arne turned toward me nervously (no more than what I felt, I'm sure), and again we looked up and down the road to make sure no one would see us. Then we got out of the car. My heart pounded, but I was ready to take on this *huge* man-swallower that at the first touch would most likely try to wrap its massive body around my neck and strangle me on the spot.

I stepped over a small ditch toward where the python lay, and it slid off in the other direction. Quick as a rabbit I bent over, grabbed it about a foot above its tail, and hung on. I was surprised at how strong it was in its struggle to get away, but I didn't loosen my grip. When writhing and struggling didn't work, the snake started hissing loudly, just like a huge housecat. It was enough to make the hair on the back of my neck stand straight up in the air, but I hung on.

When the snake realized that I wasn't about to let go, it changed tactics and whipped around to face its enemy. Of course, I never took my eyes off it even for a moment, as I knew its mouth held two or three rows of daggerlike teeth. The teeth point somewhat backward so that the snake can hold on to its prey better. Many people who've been bitten by even a small python have mistakenly yanked their hand out of its mouth, only to leave part of it inside attached to its teeth. If you're ever bitten by a python, be careful to pry open its mouth first. Only then can you remove your body part without losing too much flesh.

OK, so back to *this* snake. When it turned toward me, it seemed to get really peeved, and suddenly looked a lot bigger than it had originally. I remember seeing its mouth open really wide, and in the next instant the python almost flew across the ditch in its effort to drive those nasty teeth directly into my body. Of course, I'm no fool. I figured this might be a good time to let go and beat a hasty retreat. I leaped back over the ditch and watched as it again tried to escape in the opposite direction.

No! I couldn't let him go. Feeling quite Rambo–like at this point (even though I didn't have an AK-47 or bazooka), I jumped back toward the snake and once again grabbed its tail and hung on. This time it didn't turn and try to bite me, hissing angrily instead.

Suddenly both Arne and I heard something that almost caused our hearts to stop beating—the sound of a car. We guiltily looked up the road, and sure enough, a car was coming our direction. Even worse, it looked a lot like a ranger's vehicle. It was already quite close, so there was no use trying to jump back into our car, as whoever it was had surely seen us already. So I let go of the snake, and we did our best to look natural and relaxed, as if we'd just gotten out to stretch our legs. As the car got closer we were greatly relieved to see that it was a woman with a driver. We started to breathe again and smiled at one another as we tried to tell them about the python, but they appeared to be Kenyan and there wasn't any interest. They simply kept on driving until they were out of sight.

As soon as the coast was clear I went after the snake again. I held its tail as it wrapped its upper body around a small bush. It was breathing hard, and I knew it was wearing down fast, so I called to Arne to find a strong stick and get ready to pin down its head. Now, when I first suggested that I'd grab its tail and Arne should get its head I'd thought that I was taking the worse part of this process. But then I realized that Arne had the more challenging job, because his hands would be a lot closer to those razor-sharp teeth than mine would.

Hanging on to the tail, I watched as Arne started to sweat, trying to come up with the best way to do the inevitable without getting bitten or worse. He'd found a stick that I wasn't too sure was big enough to hold this snake's head, but he wasn't about to back down now. Oh, so carefully he pinned down its head and held it there for a few seconds to make sure it wouldn't slip from underneath the stick. Then came the real test—grabbing the snake at its head! I could tell he was quite nervous, but he went for it and got a good grip just behind the head so it couldn't reach around and enjoy a couple of tasty fingers. For my part, I kept the python's tail end as far away from its head as I could to make sure it couldn't wrap its coils around Arne. We most likely added another foot to the snake's length in our attempt to keep head and tail apart, but at last we triumphantly caught it. Victory felt great!

As we stood next to the car we decided to measure this killer, so we held it out alongside the car doors. I knew the number of inches in my hand span, so with my free hand I spread my fingers and marked off the snake's length hand by hand. You won't believe this, but once it was caught, that terrible snake shrunk to about six feet (two meters). I was quite surprised to discover that it was only as big around as my wrist as well! I figure that the original one—the one we saw out the car window—must have quickly switched places with this smaller one when we weren't looking. Maybe it happened when we were watching the car come down the road, but either way, this *was* the first python that either of us had ever caught, and I was sure that it was a lot larger at the time. Hey, my dad always did say that my eyes were bigger than my stomach! Now you see what I mean about fish and snake stories being so closely related.

After putting the snake in a jacket and closing off the armholes, I laid it across my lap, and we made our way out of the game park. We weren't going to actually steal the python, only borrow it for a couple of hours until we got some good pictures later in the afternoon. Then we'd take it back to its home. It would be resting in its own front yard before dusk.

We pulled onto the Maxwell campus, got out of the car, and walked toward Arne's house. Some of the staff kids (my own included) came running, and we told them that we had something special in the jacket, so they followed us. Arne found a big birdcage that looked plenty strong, so we carefully dumped the python into the cage, and all of us stood around admiring him for a few minutes. To tell the truth, we were feeling pretty smart. It's not every day that you get to catch a python and bring it home to show your kids. I think our kids were proud of their dads too.

It was almost time for lunch, so we decided to put the python on Arne's back porch area until we finished eating; then we'd break out the cameras. After that draining wrestling match it felt nice to put our feet up for a while and enjoy some good food. After about 30 minutes I decided the lighting was pretty good for pictures and headed up to Arne's back porch. Happy as if I had good sense, I bent down and looked inside the cage. The *empty* cage. There was no snake! I looked a bit closer and saw that one of the cage wires had been broken and the hole was just big enough for the python to escape. Then I glanced up and saw the family looking around the yard. They explained that they'd come out to see the snake, and it was gone. We figured it hadn't gone far. We assumed it had just curled itself up somewhere nearby, like maybe in the garage, which happened to be open, but incredibly the snake was nowhere to be found. We looked high and low, all over the yard. We even searched Arne's house, not to mention both adjoining yards and even my house that was next door, to no avail. Monty Python was on the loose, and it didn't look as though he was coming home any time soon!

We were all quite disappointed, to say the least. We never did find that snake. Once my son went out to feed our chickens where they lived near our backyard, and he heard a hissing sound to the right of some bushes. He thought he saw a snake, but we were never quite sure. I searched around the area and found a big hole that I thought most likely the snake had made its new home.

Arne and I caught that snake in 2001, so I figure it is probably pushing nine or 10 feet (three meters) by now, so in a way my initial guess wasn't too far off!

When I thought about this python escaping out of that strong cage, I concluded that sin is just like that snake. Think about it for a moment. Think how many people in this world believe they can hang on to sin without it destroying their lives.

I've heard people actually say that their bad (sinful) habits aren't controlling their lives, that they can drop whatever it is any time they choose. Let me assure you, it doesn't matter if it's alcohol, tobacco, pride, greed, sexual sin, hate, selfishness, or anything else in this world—the Bible is very clear that one sin cherished will keep you from God's kingdom.

Jesus implores us to grasp an important concept: "No one can serve two masters; for either he will hate the one and love the other, or else he will be loyal to the one and despise the other" (Matthew 6:24). If you or I love sin—even just one sin—and refuse to let it go, the result is eternal death. There is no way we can simultaneously serve God and consciously keep that sin. "Do you not know that a little leaven leavens the whole lump?" Paul questions his church members (1 Corinthians 5:6). Just as a little bit of yeast grows until the bread dough overflows the bowl, you can't put sin in a cage and hope it will stay put. If you keep it in your life, time and time again it will slowly but surely escape, infiltrating your mind, until in the end Satan is in complete control. And then there is no escape.

My friend, don't kid yourself. When the Ten Commandments, through the voice of the Holy Spirit, point out your sins, you had better leave them at Satan's game park, where they belong. Remember that there is a way that seems right, but the end result is death (Proverbs 14:12; 16:25). You don't believe me? Then read God's Word for yourself. That message is all through the Bible, for God wants you to understand the seriousness of sin and how much He wants you to be free.

If you seek God with a humble heart, you will see the truth about yourself. God will show you where changes need to be made, and if you want Him to do so, He will set you free.

Chapter 10

One Bad Baboon and the Mango in My Hand

When you find truth from God's Word, do not let it slip from your grasp. Guard it at all costs, because your life is at stake! Don't ever let anything go that is good, no matter how hard Satan tries to threaten or deceive you (Proverbs 4:13, PCRV; 1 Thessalonians 5:21, PCRV).

One of Kenya's more interesting animals is the baboon. Oftentimes when we drove through game parks we came upon a troop of baboons. Just like any other kind of monkey, they are quite entertaining, especially when it comes to their young. You could watch their antics for hours and hours. Not only are the young quite unattractive (I think it's quite safe to call them downright ugly, with faces only a mother can love), but they also play just like all the other "kids" in the world. In some game parks baboons are used to people and vehicles and aren't bothered in the least by an approaching car. It's quite easy to get good photos of them, as some will even jump on the hood or roof of your car, hoping to snatch some food. They're not above reaching through a window and stealing whole packages of food items, then racing down the road tearing the bag all along the way. They're quite adept at opening up almost anything.

A friend of mine, Stephen Easley, told me about his hilarious encounter with a baboon in the Nairobi Game Park. After Stephen, Terry Pottle, and another man spent the morning birding, they'd spread a blanket on the ground at a picnic site and sat down to eat lunch. They were enjoying their food when all of a sudden a large baboon came strolling out of the bushes toward them. Imagine their surprise when Mr. Baboon sat down on one corner of their blanket. He looked at them with eyebrows rising and falling as he sized up the menu.

Stephen looked at Terry. "What should we do?"

Terry responded, "I don't know what to do. What do you think we should do?"

"*I* don't know what to do!" Stephen snapped, his voice a bit high and strained.

Mr. Baboon didn't wait for them to decide what to share, but took matters into his own hands. He grabbed a jar of jam, unscrewed the lid, and proceeded to eat it. I don't remember the final outcome, but it seems that it had something to do with their chasing away the baboon and going without jam for their bread.

The reputation of the baboons that live at Nakuru National Park precedes them, so we sort of knew what to expect. We've driven down the park road in the heat of day and found baboons sprawled across it, refusing to move for us or anyone else. I have actually pulled my vehicle up to within inches of one lying in my path and still it stayed in its relaxed, reclined position. We'd heard stories about the Nakuru "bad-boons," and then one day I experienced firsthand how bad they really were.

It happened when our family was on a weekend camping trip at Nakuru. It had a fairly decent area where we could pitch our tent, and we looked forward to relaxing and having fun. We were quite excited about the trip and had planned a good menu, because everyone knows that a full stomach makes for a good time no matter what else happens. We got the tent set up and our car backed up nearby, so we decided to fix breakfast. It was one of our kids' favorite, homemade pancakes with plenty of thick syrup. My wife had brought along some large juicy mangoes, which were one of my favorite fruits to have in Africa. So we were feeling pretty satisfied as we mixed the pancake batter and cut the mangoes. Kim began frying the pancakes over our camp stove, and the kids ate them as fast as she made them. I usually waited until they'd eaten plenty before I filled my own belly.

I was relaxing at our campsite, enjoying the warmth of the sun's morning rays and breathing the fresh air, when I glanced down the road and saw a troop of baboons slowly sauntering our direction. I didn't think much about them, as up to this point we hadn't experienced anything unusual; but I continued to watch them. They were picking up things off the ground and eating whatever was edible. I was actually happy to see them, because we didn't often experience a picnic breakfast in a game park, and to see animals nearby made it even more special. As the baboons came closer and closer I figured that one of the camp guards would probably come with a stick and chase them away.

I was getting hungry, and the mangoes smelled oh-so-sweet, so I picked up a big slice and went to sit down. To my dismay, I saw that the baboons had climbed over the fence and into the camping area, and were still heading our direction. I didn't see any guards in the area, or at least didn't see any who had a club in their hands. Occupied by watching the baboons, I held the dripping mango without taking a bite. The troop came closer and still closer.

If you know anything about baboons, you will quickly remember that very large males are the protectors of the troop. When there is danger, these males do not hesitate to use their ferocity, quickness, and vicious teeth to defend the others. It has been documented that two or three big males will even kill a leopard who threatens one of their own. On many occasions I have seen their big, long teeth as they sat on a stump in the middle of the afternoon, their mouths wide open in a big yawn. Truthfully, I don't recall noticing a lot of difference between a leopard's teeth and those of a baboon.

As the troop came walking toward us I noticed that the leader was one of those big males, one of the *really* big ones. I made a mental note of an imaginary straight line from him to me, and it was uncanny how his path led directly to where I was standing. *What in the world is he coming toward me for?* I thought. I had never heard of a baboon that ate people, at least I didn't think so, but I was definitely feeling nervous. When he got within 40 feet (12 meters), I decided that it was time to make sure my family was safe, so I turned around and said, "Kids, you had better get in the car just in case." My sentence froze midway as I was surprised to see three pairs of eyes already *inside the car* staring wide-eyed out at me through rolled-up windows and behind locked doors! In the same moment Kim quickly picked up the stove and put it in the back of the car, then sort of half got in herself. What a supportive family!

So there I was, by myself, frozen in time with a sweet, dripping slice of mango in my right hand. I tell you, I'd forgotten that mango long before. It never hit me that the baboon was coming, not to eat my leg, but to get the mango. Through the whole encounter it never occurred to me. I would have gladly given it to him, if he had asked politely enough.

Thirty feet (nine meters) . . . 20 feet (six meters) . . . 15 feet (four meters) . . . By this time I was desperately searching around for some weapon, maybe a stick, a slingshot, a .22-caliber pistol, a cannon— anything to stop this baboon dead in his tracks. The only thing I could find was a plastic lid about 24" x 36" (60 centimeters x 90 centimeters). I grabbed it and held this useless thing between my tender legs and his teeth. As he got closer he suddenly opened his mouth and pulled back his lips. Saliva glistened on his Dracula-like fangs, and I just about fainted right on the spot. I glanced back at the kids, wondering if they were OK. They were pasted against the window watching Dad battle this monster and wondering how they were going to get my body back to the States when it was all over.

Then in a whirlwind Mr. Bad-boon rushed me, growling, his mouth wide open. I couldn't believe the speed of this huge thing, and before I realized what had happened he stood right next to my leg, which, you remember, was being protected by a flimsy plastic lid. Then he raced around me and stopped about 10 feet (three meters) away near the back of the car.

By this time I was sweating bullets, and Mr. Muscles had a funny look on his face, as if he hadn't eaten in five days. I braced for another attack, and I wasn't disappointed! Again he rushed me. This time I could almost feel his breath. He came so close to me that I could have easily counted his nose hairs (if I'd wanted to), but I was occupied by keeping the plastic shield between his bared teeth and my delicate skin. I couldn't figure out why no guard had come rushing to help me. I was about to be killed by a wild-eyed baboon, and nobody seemed to care. Thankfully, the rest of the troop didn't come and help him, or likely I wouldn't be here today to write this story.

After the second rush this batty baboon went on around the car, so I quickly searched the ground and found a fairly good-sized stick, which I picked up after dropping the plastic. At this point I was so angry at the whole situation that I was ready to fight.

"All right, you wanna fight? Let's do it!" I said a bit too loud, swinging the stick in a threatening manner and looking around for my attacker. But Dracula-fangs was as smart as he was vicious, and he wasn't anywhere in the vicinity! He'd seen me pick up the stick, and wisely took off toward the nearby dump located at the back of the fence. Still holding the stick, I walked over to the dump, where I'd seen the baboon disappear into a large hole. I was just about to go after him when I realized that I'd better be thankful I was still alive and standing on two unharmed legs. So I slowly walked back to the car, trying to slow my racing heart. I finally calmed down as my wife and kids came out of the vehicle. That was when I noticed that I had something in my hand. It was the mango. I took a bite, and let me assure you, it was the best-tasting mango I had ever eaten in my whole life!

This story reminds me so much of one of Satan's game plans with you and me. Jesus tells us, "I am the way, the truth, and the life. No one comes to the Father except through Me" (John 14:6). Satan knows that there is only one way out of our sinful condition. He knows it's accepting Jesus Christ as our Creator and Redeemer. Satan well knows that God's Word contains exactly what we need to gain victories against his deceptive temptations, so he does everything in his power to get us to *drop the mango,* so to speak. If Satan can keep us out of the Word of God, then he wins in the end. It's that simple. Whatever it takes to hang on to the Word of God, to study it and apply it to your life, do it at any cost.

Hang on to the mighty arm of Jesus. When you do, Satan is made helpless, and God will put him to flight with the sword of the Spirit. When Satan bares his long, jagged, temptation-filled teeth, threatening your life, remember that Jesus is coming soon. God tells you, "Hold fast what you have, that no one may take your crown" (Revelation 3:11). Nothing and nobody can separate you from Jesus. End of story.

Chapter 11

Man-eaters of Nakuru

Get serious! Don't go to sleep, because your enemy, Satan, stealthily prowls around like a hungry lion, seeking to destroy you and me. We must stay within God's camp if we will be safe from danger! (1 Peter 5:8, PCRV).

In Africa there are some things that strike fear in the hearts of everyone. Arguably, nothing causes a person to sweat more than when a man-eating lion is on the prowl in the dark of night and someone is walking through its domain with no weapon. Kenya has already been put on the map, so to speak, because of Colonel Patterson's battle against the man-eaters of Tsavo. So it takes little more than a rumor to bring back terror concerning these "ghosts in the darkness." The occasional man-eater still roams this country, lions that have killed and eaten humans, bringing sadness to the hearts of men and women and their children.

This brings me to the sad tale of a tragedy that occurred during our stay in Kenya. The place was the small game park called Nakuru, only about a two-hour drive from Nairobi. Since it is full of wildlife, it is a favorite of tourists and residents alike. Nakuru park is surrounded by an electric fence, necessary since it is located at one end of a good-sized town. Many of the usual African animals make their home inside the park, and it became our favorite place to look for leopards because many live there. Nakuru is also home to the king of beasts. When we first came to Kenya, we'd usually see them at Nakuru, sometimes even lounging on the limbs of fallen trees. Little did we know that within about two years a couple of those lions would follow in the path of their distant cousins from Tsavo.

It all started with an injury. A male in one of the prides had been injured and could hardly walk, so the park rangers felt it their duty to bring it meat every day until it was back to normal health. I suppose they couldn't stand the thought of just letting nature take its course, so they chose not to let it starve. Early each morning a ranger would drive to where this crippled lion rested and would throw out a large chunk of meat. I don't know how long this went on, but after a few weeks the lion started getting around better, and it wasn't long before it was nearly back to normal. But now there was a big problem. In the few weeks of having the ranger supply its meal the lion discovered that where there was a human, there was food. So every day the previously ill lion waited for his take-out meal, only to be disappointed when the ranger didn't come. Most likely, this lion went in search of a human *and* the meat that had been so easily obtained—no stalking, no waiting, no pouncing required.

As this was a fairly small game park, sometimes a ranger would walk from one area to another. Most of the time they carried a gun, but not always. One day a young man who'd just received his paycheck decided to go home to help his family get food and other necessities. He left the other rangers, walking across the park to another entrance/exit. A couple of days went by. He hadn't arrived home, and nobody knew where he was. A few days later someone found him, at least what was left of him. Among his badly torn clothes was found the paycheck, still in his pocket. He had been devoured by at least one lion, and possibly more. Of course, everyone involved at the park felt bad. The man had been one of their compatriots and a close friend. Besides that, they knew that they had a problem on their hands—lions that had acquired a taste for people.

The next encounter with the man-eaters left many people (including me) spellbound. One of the rangers had to go from one part of the park to another, and so began his trek. Now all the rangers knew that man-eaters were in the park, and all those who had to travel by foot kept a very close eye on their surrounding area. This man decided that it would be best if he walked along the electric fence (inside the park, of course), as it would be more unlikely that the lions would spend very much time near the powerful voltage.

Before I go any further, let me describe the fence so that you will understand the rest of the story. The electric wires are approximately 10 to 12 inches (25 to 30 centimeters) apart, and the fence is more than eight feet (two and a half meters) tall. The rangers have the electricity set to a voltage that will knock out any animal or human for about two hours but won't kill them.

So the ranger began his trek and was making pretty good time. I'm sure he kept a wary eye on any tawny animals that happened to be in the area. As he strode along he suddenly heard a noise behind him. He turned, and what he saw caused him to freeze in his tracks! The ranger saw something that few human beings have ever seen and lived to tell about it. Two male lions were running directly toward him, and they weren't coming for a friendly visit. About 100 yards (a little less than 100 meters) behind him came the man-eaters, who thought they had happened upon their next meal and were coming in for the kill! The ranger took off at top speed, as fast as his legs could go. His life depended upon it! As Kenyans are fantastic long-distance runners, this man most likely kept up a world-record pace that would have made his country proud had it been on Olympic soil. But no matter how fast a human can run, it is never fast enough to outrun a hungry lion. For a short distance they can run more than 50 miles (80 kilometers) per hour.

The man's mind raced, along with his legs, as he desperately tried to think of some way to save his life. The lions quickly closed the gap as the man peered over his shoulder. Two hundred fifty feet (75 meters), 200 feet (60 meters), 165 feet (50 meters), 130 feet (40 meters). Just as the man-eaters closed the gap to 100 feet (30 meters), an idea popped into the ranger's head. He had only one chance, and that was it. His plan couldn't fail, or he would lose his life. He would attempt to dive through the wires of the electric fence. He knew that he would be instantly knocked out and wouldn't know if he had succeeded until a couple of hours had passed. And if he didn't succeed? At least he wouldn't be conscious to feel himself forced to the ground, his neck crushed between the jaws of a huge lion.

Sixty-five feet (20 meters).

Thirty-three feet (10 meters).

Now!

The young man took quick mental note of the distance between the wires and threw himself in the direction of the largest open space, about chest-high.

About two hours later he slowly opened his eyes. Looking around, he saw that he lay *outside* the electric fence. Praise the Lord, his life had been spared. As he sat up, something caught his attention, and he felt his heart almost stop beating. Just on the other side of the fence stood the lions licking their chops, looking wistfully at the ranger, disappointed that they'd lost their meal. Let me tell you, this man most assuredly thanks God every day that he is still alive and able to go home to his family. What an amazing ending to what could have been another tragedy in Nakuru.

Unfortunately, this wasn't the end of the road for these vicious man-eaters. It wasn't too long before they struck again. The sun had just set as the two demons loped to the rangers' homes near the front entrance of the park. Dusk is the usual time that lions begin to stir, as their stomachs demand more food. They have nocturnal vision, and at dusk can see as well as we can in the daylight. The lions, already with the taste of human flesh in their blood, quietly padded up to the homes, figuring they had a good chance of finding a meal. Often the rangers got together in the evenings, visiting until bed-time, and this evening was no exception. A group of them were talking and laughing at one of their homes as the lions stealthily crept closer and closer. Lions are very patient, and will oftentimes wait up to a couple of hours to make sure that they make a kill.

Sometime later one unfortunate female ranger left the house to get a blanket. The lions crept behind her, not making a sound. She went into her house, got the blanket, and headed back toward where the group was hanging out. She never made it. The lions attacked, knocking her to the ground. She screamed, of course. She screamed for her life, but one of the lions grabbed her by the throat, and that was the end. Hearing her scream, the other rangers grabbed their guns and raced outside. They shot into the air to frighten the

135

lions away, and the beasts disappeared into the darkness. The rangers raced to the stricken woman, only to find that she was gone.

What a horrible way to die, in the mouth of a lion. I often wonder why the rangers didn't shoot the man-eaters sooner, but until then they weren't sure which *were* the man-eaters, and they surely didn't want to kill them all. Needless to say, it didn't take long for them to kill a number of lions, the man-eaters' pride.

What a devastating story. A few times when we'd entered the park my family and I had seen that last victim *alive,* but now she was gone! What a senseless tragedy. Those lions of Nakuru remind me of another man-eater. The Bible calls him Satan, that old serpent called the devil. God's Word has a lot to say about him. First Peter 5:8 warns us, "Be sober, be vigilant; because your adversary the devil walks about like a roaring lion, seeking whom he may devour." Satan has gotten the taste of human flesh more than once or twice. Yes, thousands and thousands of times has he prowled around looking for his next victim. How many times has this devious lion grabbed a human being by the throat, causing that life to ebb away? How many victims has Satan devoured because they didn't stay within God's fence of biblical truth? Only God knows the answer to that question, and we will have to wait to find out when we get to heaven. But the fact remains that you don't have to be his next meal. You, my friend, can be safe from him forever. Just do as James 4:7, 8 says: "Resist the devil and he will flee from you. Draw near to God and He will draw near to you." He will protect you with His powerful voltage of omnipotence. Enter the camp of the Lion of the tribe of Judah. He is all-loving, all-powerful, all-everything, Jesus Christ! He is the one who once long ago let Satan grip His throat. He became a bleeding victim of that roaring lion so that you and I wouldn't have to feel his bone-crushing grip! Stay in God's fence, and Satan can't touch your eternity with Jesus. But if you choose to remain outside God's protection you will be stalked by that man-eater or one of his pride, and sooner or later your life will end, forever! The choice is yours. Remember it's the truth that will set you free. That truth is found in the Bible and through prayer to the Almighty One. If you desire to live, He will show you the way.

Chapter 12

Students Who Chose Jesus Over Mom and Dad

Don't think that I came to bring peace on earth. I also carry a sword! For I am come to set a man at variance against his father, and the daughter against her mother, and the daughter-in-law against her mother-in-law. And a man's enemies shall be those in his own house. He who loves father or mother more than Me is not worthy of Me; and he that loves son or daughter more than Me is not worthy of Me. When Mom and Dad go against Me, your only safety is with Me. You must choose between us (Matthew 10:34-37, PCRV).

W hat would you do if you happened across a truth in God's Word that you felt you must embrace, but your mom and dad and brother and sister stood in your way? What if, in fact, they actually placed barriers in front of you to discourage you from moving outside of the realm of "normal" family religious values and traditions? What if your family threatened to physically prevent you from following God's Word or threatened to banish you from their home forever? Would you choose to follow what you felt the Bible was telling you to, or would you comply with Mom and Dad?

I was blessed to be reared in a Seventh-day Adventist home with Christian parents, two Christian sisters and a Christian brother. If you had asked me during my teenage years if I understood how blessed I was to be born into my family, I would have probably shrugged and said something typical—but not without sincerity— such as "Sure, I'm glad I was born into this home. I couldn't ask for any better parents, sisters, and brother than my own." The truth is that back then I didn't have a clue how privileged I really was. Today I rejoice that the good Lord has placed some spiritual salve on my eyes that has helped me more clearly see how fortunate I was to have the freedom to become a Seventh-day Adventist.

During my six years pastoring at Maxwell the Lord began to open my eyes to the reality of what it means to be raised in an Adventist home, as each school year brought a number of students from non-Adventist homes. Now, I knew that it's not always a good thing for private Christian schools to open their doors to students who do not share the same beliefs and ideals. There is a legitimate concern that worldly influences might infiltrate the young Christian minds instead of the Christian minds infiltrating the worldly-minded. As an elementary school teacher and a pastor I have mostly supported that philosophy and stood firmly against opening doors very wide because of the unknown variables behind them. I whole-heartedly believe that as parents, teachers, and pastors we get one chance with our children and we can't blow it.

But I recall sitting with the principal during my first year at Maxwell, discussing this very subject as we added up how many kids without an Adventist background were attending the school. Then Arne Nielsen, looking serious but with a slight smile and a twinkle in his eyes, said eight words that embedded themselves into my mind: "We can look at this as an opportunity!"

From that point on I had a new purpose. I realized that with God's guiding hand and a spiritual staff and student body we could take this opportunity and run with it.

Throughout my first four years there I could see the hand of God working on the hearts of many of the students, especially the ones that did not have an Adventist background. In any church or religious organization it takes a concerted effort to witness, share truth, and guide individuals to choose Jesus and stand with God's remnant through baptism.

It was fascinating to watch the spiritual growth of certain students through their contact with Christian teachers. I'm talking about more than the Bible teachers. I'm speaking of teachers who shared Jesus during math, history, English, science, computer classes, and yes, even physical education, not to forget the influence of the dormitory deans. You teachers who don't happen to teach Bible classes don't ever underestimate God's ability to use you to witness in your classroom. I guarantee that if you pray and if you look for opportunities—being willing to not always cover material you'd previously planned—God will open wide the spiritual doors. Remember that at least one thing is more important than academics, and that is Jesus Christ. It's a sad situation when any Christian teacher thinks that finishing the day's lesson plan is all that really matters. When I compare the miracle of a student accepting Christ with all the classes in the world, the classes don't even come close in importance. Teachers would do well to forget classwork once in a while and open up for discussion about Jesus and the truth from God's Word instead.

Sometimes a student would come to the cafeteria with a downcast look. "How are you doing?" I'd ask. "Why the long face?"

"Pastor Curt, I just got a D on my chemistry test."

So I'd tell the student, "Hey, I have good news for you! Did you try your very best on the test?"

The answer was usually yes.

"Then why are you so down?" I'd ask. "God still loves you, and just because you flunked that test doesn't change God's mind. It has nothing to do with your salvation. Whether you got an A or an F on a test, God still loves you, and heaven is still your home. You have reason to celebrate!"

Yes, academics are important. It's important to study for a test and do homework. It's important to develop good study skills and good habits in life. But we have to keep all things in perspective. The bottom line is that when God draws each one to Himself to save us, He doesn't look at our past spiritual track record and definitely not our academic one. I can just see it now. You arrive at heaven's gate, and just as you're about to enter, Gabriel stops you and says, "Hey, wait a second. Didn't you flunk a test in the tenth grade in

Mr. Dull's class? Sorry, you can't come in here. Heaven's only for really smart people!"

I had good news for our students, and I have good news for you. God doesn't care anything about your academic record—only your surrender to Jesus Christ!

Not only were the staff a vital part of witnessing to all of our kids, but who can underestimate the value of fellow Christian students! I found a wonderful statement in a tremendously valuable book, *Messages to Young People*. "Satan is a vigilant foe, intent upon his purpose of leading the youth to a course of action entirely contrary to that which God would approve. He well knows that *there is no other class that can do as much good as young men and young women who are consecrated to God*. The youth, if right, could sway a mighty influence. Preachers, or laymen advanced in years, cannot have one-half the influence upon the young that the youth, devoted to God, can have upon their associates" (p. 204; italics supplied).

I remember an Ethiopian student named Befkru, affectionately called Buff by his classmates. Here was a young man who had never even heard of God or Jesus, let alone that He had come to earth to live with sinful humans and then died so we may have eternal life. Within two years—mainly because of our student prayer warriors who daily moved the hand of God in Buff's behalf, and the spiritual influence of Alex, his friend and fellow student, a young man truly devoted to God—Befkru accepted Jesus Christ as his personal Savior and was baptized. Before he left Maxwell, Befkru told me "I never knew God before, but now when I do something wrong I feel God speaking to me in my heart and I feel bad."

What a testimony for God's amazing ability to use dedicated youth to reach an atheistic-minded teenager. Surely we can triumphantly declare, "Behold, the Lord's hand is not shortened, that it cannot save" (Isaiah 59:1).

It was during the 2003-2004 school year that God decided to open my eyes to the privilege of growing up in a Seventh-day Adventist home. On campus were six young people for whom the Lord was working mightily. Each of these teens had come from

Christian, but not Adventist, homes. Little did they know, when they first stepped foot on campus, that God had His wonderful plan in motion, gently pursuing them to accept more truth and drawing them "out of Babylon" to stand with His people. Had they known the choice they would face, they might have shrunk from the task.

It was a beautiful Kenyan Sabbath morning when six young people responded to the Holy Spirit's invitation to be baptized, and came up to the front of the church. I looked over the congregation and saw tears of joy and faces filled with happiness at these decisions. And as I thought back on their lives during the past year or two, it was simply amazing how the Holy Spirit had changed their hearts and convicted them to follow God's Word. How thankful I was for the influence of teachers, students, and the Holy Spirit.

Of course, I knew that Satan wouldn't give up so easily, and for four of these students the battle had just begun. From past experience I knew that when the battle started, the campus prayer warriors had to stay busy day and night! We must remember that even with all of our human efforts nothing is possible without the Spirit of God. " 'Not by might nor by power, but by *My Spirit,*' says the Lord of hosts" (Zechariah 4:6).

The apostle Paul, too, was very familiar with the vital power of prayer. Ephesians 6:18 commands us to pray for each other "always with all prayer and supplication in the Spirit, being watchful to this end with all perseverance and supplication for all the saints." I knew that we must persevere through prayer for these students, and pray those mighty prayer warriors did! Without their prayers, I am sure that Satan would have discouraged these six students into rejecting Jesus and their newfound truth.

Hanan, one of the young women, battled with a looming threat from her Greek Orthodox mother who carried Arabic influences. Her mom said that Hanan would no longer be her daughter if she was baptized into the Seventh-day Adventist church. Hanan and her mother were very close to each other, and you can imagine the terrible struggle Hanan went through.

Nami was determined to follow in her brother's footsteps (from the year before) in spite of her parents' refusal to support her in any way. They would not attend her baptism, and were quite unhappy with her decision.

Danny, the lone gentleman of the group, asked for baptism after his parents agreed to support his decision. But when they realized how serious he was and that he would be keeping the seventh-day Sabbath, they were distressed. They informed the school administration that now their son would feel guilt because he had to choose between his family and his religious beliefs. It would be an ongoing problem, they said, and it would cause a lot of friction in the family. They added that they wished they had been in on Danny's decision and had understood what it meant to be baptized into the Adventist Church.

Jesus said almost exactly the same thing as did Danny's parents. Instructing His disciples, Jesus told them, "For I am come to set a [young] man at variance against his father, and the daughter against her mother. . . . And a man's foes shall be they of his own household" (Matthew 10:35, 36, KJV).

Only after Natalie's decision to be baptized did she talk to her parents about it. It was the last week of school, and she and they discussed it throughout the week. Her parents were most upset and told her that under no circumstances was she to go through with it. Her stepfather went so far as to threaten that if she tried to be baptized he would come and physically take her away. She was very scared, but later in the week she again asked them for permission. Again they gave an emphatic no.

Natalie came to me that very Friday of the planned evening baptism and said that she had decided to wait until next year, when she would be 18 and free to do what she wanted. I told her that I would support her decision, but I felt sad and heavyhearted. Leaving her, I walked to the ad building, praying for her as I walked. It seemed that Satan had won this battle, and I implored for God to intervene.

Little did I realize that God's arsenal against the forces of Satan weren't depleted in the least. God had planned ahead, and He was just getting warmed up. Twenty minutes later Natalie came running across the campus toward me. I was walking toward her, hardly daring for good news, when she blurted out, "Pastor Curt, I've changed my mind. I want to get baptized tonight with the others!"

I stared in disbelief, almost not believing this sudden change. Finally after what seemed a few minutes, I asked, "Why did you change your mind, Natalie?"

Her answer will forever burn in my heart. "Pastor Curt, when you left after I said that I was going to wait until next year, I went into the dorm. Suddenly I remembered something you'd said in a sermon. It was something like 'He or she who loves father or mother more than Me is not worthy of Me.'" Then with the most sincere face I had seen in a long time, Natalie looked at me and said, "I just want to put God first."

Tears came to my eyes as I told her that we would carry through with the baptism. I went away completely humbled by the awesome power of God. Truly "with God all things are possible." I could hardly contain myself! All the way home I felt like praising the Lord for this almost supernatural demonstration of His loving power. Maybe this feeling I had was something like Paul's when he asked with utmost confidence, "If God is for us, who can be against us?" (Romans 8:31). Don't you just love his God-inspired answer? "For I am persuaded that neither death nor life, nor angels nor principalities nor powers, nor things present nor things to come, nor height nor depth, nor any other created thing, shall be able to separate us from the love of God which is in Christ Jesus our Lord" (verses 38, 39).

I praise the Lord that Natalie's parents didn't show up at the baptism and drag her away. But even if they had, it comforts my heart to know that Natalie and the other students were willing to stand for the truth from God's Word and, ultimately, to put Jesus first no matter the outcome. During the next school year Natalie told me that when her parents learned that she had been baptized, they respected her for her decision. Another answer to prayer! What a mighty God we serve! *"And everyone who has left houses or brothers or sisters or father or mother or wife or children or lands, for My name's sake, shall receive a hundredfold, and inherit eternal life"* (Matthew 19:29).

Now, I understand how blessed I was to be born into a Seventh-day Adventist family. Hardly a day goes by that I don't think about Natalie and those other students and how they chose Jesus and God's way over Mom and Dad. I praise Him for the wonderful privilege He bestowed upon me. I also thank God that I see a bit more clearly what it means to really sacrifice for Him, what it means to give up this world and everything and everybody in it.

Jesus said, "Whoever confesses Me before men, him I will also confess before My Father who is in heaven" (Matthew 10:32). I can't help asking myself, "If I had been in Natalie's shoes, would I have had the courage to make the same decision?" I don't know the answer, and I thank God I don't have to make that choice. But for those who do have to choose today whom you will serve, I have something very important for you. It is this promise from your heavenly Father, who loves you with all His heart: "Fear not, for I am with you; Be not dismayed, for I am your God. I will strengthen you, Yes, I will help you, I will uphold you with My righteous right hand" (Isaiah 41:10).

Chapter 13

You Can Take the Man Out of Kenya . . .

For God so loves Kenyans, Americans, and every other nationality in this world that Jesus willingly and unhesitatingly offered His life to save us all, because we are all His children regardless of color, sex, or culture. He loves us all equally and has an overwhelming desire that we surrender our lives to our Savior, that we love and accept each other as brothers and sisters, and that we take up our cross and follow Jesus to our eternal home in heaven (John 3:16, PCRV).

There's an old saying that I have heard often from people who've been missionaries in Kenya. It goes like this. *You can take the man out of Kenya, but you can never take Kenya out of the man.* I don't know who it was that first came up with this conclusion, but I know from experience that it is the truth.

As I previously implied, before living in Kenya, I thought that the United States of America was the only important country in the world. I had that typical American attitude that we were the best and that every place and everyone else was subservient. Looking back at those narrow-minded days, I can see that I was truly blind as a bat! I was looking through one very small pair of dark glasses, completely oblivious to how large and important the rest of the world is—especially to God. Come to think of it, reading the Genesis account of Creation, I don't recall that God made one piece of land more important than any other. I've never read anywhere in the Bible that U.S. citizens are more special or greater loved than those in Kenya, Nigeria, Norway, Chile, Great Britain, or anywhere else. The only thing I've learned is that God so loved the *world!*

I am thankful for the years I spent in Kenya for many reasons. But I am most thankful for the eyedrops God placed in my eyes so that I could see an important truth. To a Kenyan, Kenya is most special, even if many would like the opportunity for a better life in a developed country. To a Filipino, the Philippines are the greatest. To a Canadian, Canada is the best. To an Egyptian, Egypt is supreme. To an American, the United States is the home of choice. Everyone should be proud of their country and of their roots. Since God made the whole world, there should be room enough for all of us to have national pride without thinking that we are better than other people who happen to live in some other country. God is the one who made us who we are. God is the Creator who gave us our distinctive characters, color, and physical characteristics, so everyone should strive to be the best in spite of our sinful state.

Sometimes people ask me, "What color do you think God is?" Another question I've entertained more than once is "What color do you think we will be when we get to heaven?"

Whatever color God is, it will represent purity, love, and righteousness and, I assure you, have nothing to do with which race is the best. Whatever color God chooses for you and me will reflect perfect beauty and the rich tint of health and Christ's righteousness. We must get out of majoring in minors and get back to the powerful gospel message found in that song of old. *Red and Yellow, Black and White, all are precious in His sight, Jesus loves the little [and big] children of the world.*

Before our journey through Kenya I would often hear national anthems being played or sung, but I didn't pay much attention to them because they weren't my national song. But now when I hear a national anthem from any country I try to remember to stand respectfully and quietly, because that country is respected and important to some of my own brothers and sisters in the world. Maybe they are longing for their homeland, just as I longed for mine so many times while living in Kenya. Their national anthem brings goose bumps to their arms, just as "The Star-Spangled Banner" does to mine, and that's the way it should be.

My six years living in Kenya taught me more about life than I had learned in the previous 33. Wherever I go I will, forever, remember Kenya—its people, its animals, and its way of life. The people living there are something special. Kenyans are very friendly and will talk to you on the streets. *Hacuna matata* is their motto in life: No problems, no worries. When you greet a Kenyan, even for a business venture, you don't start talking business right away. To do so is considered very rude. A Kenyan knows what's really important, and that is family and loved ones. This might be a typical conversation when two people meet.

"*Jambo! Habari?*" (Hello! How are you?)

"*Mzuri Sana.*" (I am very fine.)

"And how is your family?"

"My family is doing very fine. My eldest daughter is in form 3 now and doing very well."

"How is your wife? I heard she was sick last week."

"My wife is much improved and has already gone back to work."

"You are looking very fat [a compliment in Kenya, believe it or not!] and healthy. God is treating you well, eh?"

"Ah, *asante sana*. Thank you very much. You are very kind."

"And how are your mother and father?"

It's tough for a normal "gotta run" American to come to Kenya and suddenly slow down to first gear. What a blessing it is, though. America and other industrialized countries could take a lesson from this. Their people would probably live about 20 years longer if they followed the mentality of Kenya and other similar countries.

If you were to drive down the road any morning, you might see a large number of nicely dressed Kenyans standing by the roadside. As you travel back up the same road that evening, you would most likely see the same Kenyans standing in the same spots. Jobs are very hard to come by for the majority of Kenyans, and so for many their lives consist of getting dressed and going out by the road and doing absolutely nothing but talking to passersby. They dress nicely, often with bright colors, the brighter the better. Being so culturally friendly, Kenyans frequently talk to others, and it doesn't necessarily matter whether they know each other or not. This has been a great blessing for Maxwell Academy when it comes to outreach on Sabbath afternoons. Sharing Jesus with a Kenyan is very easy, for they are very cordial. They ask questions and hardly ever pass up an opportunity to take some literature. When you have nothing, it's very easy to accept Jesus and what He has to offer.

Some mannerisms in Kenya wouldn't sit too well with Americans. For example, it is not unusual to see two men, any age, standing together holding hands in an intimate sort of way. This means nothing but "I like your friendship, and I think of you as a good friend." It took me five years to get used to this. Even though I knew and understood the way of their culture, it took a long time for my mind to let go of its American mentality. In the United States if I tried to show my friendship by holding another guy's hand, I'd most likely be immediately decked by a left hook.

Besides the friendly hand holding, Kenyans aren't afraid to enter each other's personal space. The normal space I like to keep to my-self is a radius of about three and one-half feet (one meter). Kenyans will often split that in half, and sometimes come even closer, until you are nose to nose or eyeball to eyeball! Let me tell you, it's not the country to live in if you have a phobia of people.

One of the customs I actually enjoy is that of staring at other people. Even in America I think that we'd all like to stare at others. People are fascinating to watch, so what's so wrong with giving a stare? In fact, many people actually dress in strange ways, hoping that they get attention. Right? It's strange that as much as Americans would like to stare, those same people get angry if someone else stares at them. One of my favorite sayings in the States used to be "Hey, buddy, why don't you take a picture? It'll last a lot longer!" But the fact still remains that if you value your life in the States, either you look when their back is turned or you don't look at all. In Kenya you can look at anyone to your heart's content. Kenyans will not get mad. On the contrary, they'll often stare right back at you for as long as they like. They aren't being rude and disrespectful, but I admit it feels a bit weird, as if they are looking into your mind and reading your thoughts.

The kids in Kenya are pretty special too. Even the children who don't have much schooling know three English words, *How are you?* They will say these words with an emphasis on the last word so it sounds like this: "How are *you?*" I've had lots of fun answering them in Swahili, prompting immediate giggles and ear-to-ear grins.

By far the toughest thing to deal with is their asking for money. During our last year in Kenya things got so bad that I had to tell the Maxwell receptionist that I was no longer receiving phone calls. Some days I'd get five or six calls from people who wanted *counseling* from the pastor. Word gets around when you help someone out financially. I have had people from Uganda, Sudan, and Tanzania come to my door asking for help. The sad part is that most are genuine needs. The need usually concerns school fees, food to eat, travel fare to get home, or the death of a loved one. Little did I know that what was called the death of a mom could mean any of the following: a grandma, great-grandma, mother, husband's mother, cousin's mother, aunt, aunt's mother, or husband's father's daughter's mother. One week a young woman came to us saying that she needed money to bury her mother, so we gave her a couple thousand shillings. About a month later she came again. This time she said that she had lost her mother.

"Now, wait a second," I said. "I thought you already lost your mother."

"Oh, no. That was my sister's mother. This is my husband's mother."

On a sadder note is the overwhelming problem of AIDS. Every day hundreds of people in Kenya die of AIDS. Some towns right near Maxwell have a ratio of one in five people who are carriers of HIV. It broke my heart when an obviously sick father came to my door asking for money to take his children back to his tribal home so his family could take care of them when he died. I've had the sick bring their medical papers proving that what they say is, in fact, true, and by the looks of some they don't have much time left.

More than once I have had an 8- or 10-year-old friend from nearby come to my door, weeping because their beloved mom just died of AIDS. These faces are forever etched in my memory and will haunt me until Jesus comes. Oh, that those with money would open their hearts to give to those less fortunate than themselves. So many needs! So few willing hearts that could bring Jesus to so many starving souls.

To see kids of all ages living on the streets, often hungry, their tattered clothes just hanging on their skinny frames, is enough to tear your heart out. These street kids may go without food for days. Many times we bought bread and milk and gave it to a small boy, only to see an older boy snatch it away and stuff his own mouth as he raced around a corner.

How disheartening it is to see money spent on extravagant things such as an expensive new car or maybe a new inground pool when in Kenya (and many other places) Seventh-day Adventist brothers and sisters are meeting under a tree in town because they have no church. How the love of most has grown cold, especially in my own country! How can we let the poor suffer day after day, often without so much as lifting one finger to help them? How can our spiritual leadership spend thousands of dollars for unnecessarily large homes or new extravagant office buildings when there are church members, *our own people,* who don't know where their next meal is coming from? We walk around claiming the title Seventh-day Adventist Christian, yet continue to look out for number one instead of truly loving one another. "By this all will know that you are my disciples, if you have love for one another" (John 13:35).

In numerous ways God has instructed us to take care of the poor, fatherless, and widows. Are we doing our part, or are we failing? Go to Kenya and decide for yourself. Oh, that God would intervene and bring about what happened in the days of the early Christian church. Acts 2:44-47 reminds us of our God-given duty to our fellow men and the blessings that will follow. "Now all who believed were together, and had all things in common [belongings open to all], and sold their possessions and goods, and divided them among all, as anyone had need. So continuing daily with one accord in the temple, and breaking bread from house to house, they ate their food with gladness and simplicity of heart, praising God and having favor with all the people. And the Lord added to the church daily those who were being saved."

If we had this same spirit of giving today, Jesus would most assuredly come quickly! Remember: *where your treasure is, there will your heart be also*.

How can anyone say enough about the wildlife in this place? When it comes to animals, there is no place like Kenya. Income from tourism to view the native animals is what keeps this country's head above water. The government usually goes to great lengths to protect the wild animals. During our six years in Kenya we saw so many impressive animals that it's hard to rate one over the other. But I will not soon forget the one that carries the title Big Daddy! This crocodile is truly a monster, weighing in at more than 1,800 pounds (670 kilograms). From the tip of his nose to the end of his tail he measures more than 16 feet (five meters). Before he was captured and brought to a coastal place called Mamba village, he had eaten five or six men near the Tana River. He now spends most of his time in a small pond, but when crowds are taken around to see the different crocodiles they always end with Big Daddy.

Our first time to witness this mammoth left us openmouthed with awe. People surrounded his pen. Cameras were poised over the fence. Then one of our guides grabbed a big piece of cow meat and, shaking it over the fence, began to call him. We saw his head rise to the surface as he swam toward the pond's edge. Then in a burst of energy Big Daddy exploded out of the water and onto the bank. His mouth wide open, he hurtled toward the meat.

It seemed that everyone held their breath while their eyeballs popped as if they would fall right out! Then the cameras started flashing, and "oohs" and "ahhhs" resounded through the crowd. There are really no words to explain the gigantic size of Big Daddy, but of this I am sure, I will never forget that croc.

As time came for us to leave Kenya, Kim and I had a difficult time deciding which we would miss more—the people or the animals. The feeling that comes into our hearts when we fondly remember our encounters with wild animals is worth more than gold. I can't readily explain it, but quite frequently my heart burns within me with an almost overwhelming desire to go back to the wild. You've heard of *the call of the wild*. Perhaps it is something like that.

I don't know why, but my heart physically hurt when I thought of moving away from Kenya, of moving far from the people and animals. It created an emotional pain that was almost as if I were moving far away from my own family. The memories created while in the game parks will always be with me.

I will never forget the time in the Masai Mara when we hung a baseball cap tied to a rope out of our car window. With the rope and cap we played tug-of-war with two young cheetahs that came to our car door while Mama watched from a short distance away. What a feeling of exhilaration coursed through my blood as I felt their strength during the game.

Another everlasting memory happened in the Nairobi Game Park when we saw two mother lions with seven younger ones. We'd seen the young ones from time to time, and watched as they grew until they were about two thirds the size of the adults. One day I came up with a *brilliant* idea. I would tie one of Ashley's old teddy bears to a fairly long rope, throw it out the car window, and see if one of the young lions would grab the end of it. Wrapping the other end of the rope around my hands a number of times, I waited, little realizing the strength of even a partially grown lion. One of the young males grabbed that bear and immediately yanked backwards, nearly severing my fingers. I couldn't believe the strength of that furry friend! It was fortunate that I was able to quickly unwind the rope and let it go, for the lion took off with a 40-foot (12-meter) rope dragging behind him, and six other cubs chasing the end of it! I drove after him until he let go of the bear, and then quickly got out and grabbed the end of the rope. This time I wrapped the rope around the steering wheel and then threw the bear toward the lions.

Again, Mr. Tough Guy grabbed it and yanked so hard that the steering wheel actually turned about a quarter turn.

One of our most awesome encounters with animals occurred right on the campus of Maxwell Adventist Academy. Our telephone rang early one morning near graduation weekend. One of the students excitedly said that there was a leopard or cheetah near the court area and asked if I could come. I didn't need a second invitation! I jumped out of bed with my wife close on my heels, and we pulled on some clothes and ran down to the court area. Early that morning two of the students, Esperant Mulumba and Illari Ribeyro, had been sitting on a bench, studying for a final test. Another student, Paul Mwansa, lounged on the dorm porch. Suddenly Espy looked up and saw a strange-looking dog slowly jogging next to the dorm, heading toward the cafeteria. As he squinted against the somewhat dark morning light, he asked Illari if she could see it. As they watched the animal continuing toward the cafeteria, all three figured out that this was no dog at all. It was a beautiful full-grown male cheetah who'd been enticed to Maxwell by the Thompson gazelle that lived on campus. When Kim and I got down by the court, we saw him sitting up near the fence just across the road from my court office. I couldn't believe my eyes. It was far beyond awesome. It's not every day, even in Africa, that a cheetah pops in to say hello. Before long all the juniors and seniors as well as the staff had come out to join the circus.

Two hours and about five phone calls later, park rangers came with their dart gun so they could safely take Spot back to the game park. Now, I'm not sure whether one of the rangers had ever had the opportunity to stalk a cheetah before, or if he was just plain scared. But even with Dean Edwards, our technology director, giving direction from the top of a nearby tree, this poor guy didn't seem to have a clue. Now, it doesn't take a rocket scientist to figure out that if you keep your dart gun at your shoulder pointing in the direction of the cat and your eyes are looking that same direction too, your chances for success are much greater.

However, this ranger had his own philosophy. I watched, incredulous, as he walked toward the cheetah, the rifle at his waist pointing toward the ground and his eyes looking in every direction but at the cat. When he was about 10 or 12 feet (three or four meters) away I thought to myself, *There's no way anyone could miss that close*. But while the ranger looked to the left, the cat jumped up and ran to the right toward the chicken coop down along the fence line.

The ranger quickly jogged closer and fired the dart. The cheetah, figuring it was time to head for the Acacia hills, took off toward the top of the campus, with nearly half the school running after him. One ranger yelled that the cheetah had been hit and wouldn't last more than about two minutes, so we eyeballed him as best we could until he disappeared behind the Dulls' house. Camera in hand, I raced to the backyard until I came to the side of Lloyd's electric fence, scanning everywhere, looking for a fainting cheetah. Imagine my surprise as I glanced to the other side of the yard and saw Mr. Spot, and he wasn't anywhere close to going night-night! There he sat, not more than 40 feet (12 meters) away, staring at me. He looked very afraid.

I hit my video camera's record button as he took off running across the back field, down to the lower part of campus where our home was located. I got some unbelievable footage—poetry in motion. There is not much else quite as impressive as a cheetah at a full run. Quickly running after him, I met the ranger with gun in hand, who informed me that the dart had bounced off the cheetah and never penetrated his skin. *Wonderful!* I thought. I may not have gotten quite so close if I had known that fact. (I found out later that there is no record of a cheetah ever attacking a human.) We silently crept around the front of my home to the side yard. I noticed that the ranger had finally figured out the process as he kept the gun up near his eye the whole time, as if he were in some SWAT movie hunting down a big-time murderer. As we carefully peered over our bushes he quickly raised the gun, only to drop it to his waist. The cheetah was standing right below our bedroom window.

"Man, this is really cool. A cheetah right in our own yard! It doesn't get any better than this!" I said to myself, shaking my head in amazement. But in a heartbeat he took off again. We ran after him, but he jumped the fence and went back up on campus. Unfortunately for the cheetah, he disappeared into the trees. We were all disappointed, but hopefully he found his way back into the game park. We never saw him again.

This is truly what Africa is all about. In the animal world and with people, just when you think you've seen everything, God brings another blessing your way. I thank Him often for the experiences that graced our lives during our six years there. The best way I can respond is "What a country!" and "What a God!" I wouldn't trade those years for anything, for there was never a dull moment. My life will never be the same. Oh, that our universities and colleges would require every student to take one year off to serve as a missionary somewhere else in the world. Then our students would be truly educated in God's way. This is something it's hard to get in a campus classroom—a realization that God loves every person in this world with all His heart, that He loves each the same as anyone else! Jesus would have us open our arms, encompassing our brothers and sisters with all the love we can muster.

My eyes have been opened as I have seen God miraculously lead my life from beginning to end. From my mother's death until we left Kenya, God was in control. He moved in mysterious ways to bring about His will for my life. The truth is that through my *entire* life He was *always* in control, even though I was often oblivious to His presence. He can be in control of *your* life if you *choose this day whom you will serve.*

Give God a chance and surrender everything to Him. Then fasten your seat belt and remember that even though bad times come your way, those stressing times are directly in God's hands. Someday soon you'll understand the purpose they served in your life. Trust God implicitly, and I assure you, you won't be disappointed. Maybe someday Kenya, or another special country, will become part of you. Who knows the mind and the mysterious ways of God! If you've got the guts, God will get the glory as souls are brought to the kingdom! "Choose for yourselves this day. . . . As for me and my house, we will serve the Lord" (Joshua 24:15).

Who knows? Maybe one day you, too, will look around and exclaim, "Wow! I can't believe I'm in Africa!"

YOUR NEXT GREAT READ

Under the Shadow

Mary Hui-Tze Wong
with Maylan Schurch

Enter a story packed with adventure and challenge, peril and plague, and bombs raining from the sky. This is the incredible true story of two people who searched for God, heard His call to service, and discovered His unfailing providence and miraculous leading. 0-8280-1938-X. Paperback, 128 pages.

3 WAYS TO SHOP

- Visit your local ABC
- Call 1-800-765-6955
- www.AdventistBookCenter.com